Arab Marxism and National Liberation

Historical Materialism Book Series

VOLUME 223

The titles published in this series are listed at *brill.com/hm*

Arab Marxism and National Liberation

Selected Writings of Mahdi Amel

Introduced and edited by

Hicham Safieddine

Translated by

Angela Giordani

BRILL

LEIDEN | BOSTON

The Library of Congress Cataloging-in-Publication Data is available online at http://catalog.loc.gov
LC record available at http://lccn.loc.gov/2020040667

Typeface for the Latin, Greek, and Cyrillic scripts: "Brill". See and download: brill.com/brill-typeface.

ISSN 1570-1522
ISBN 978-90-04-44423-2 (hardback)
ISBN 978-90-04-44424-9 (e-book)

This book is printed on acid-free paper and produced in a sustainable manner.

For Evelyne Brun Hamdan (1937–2020)

∵

You are not defeated as long as you resist.

MAHDI AMEL (Beirut, 1982)

∵

Contents

Foreword IX
Gilbert Achcar
Acknowledgements XII
Note on Translation XIV

PART 1
Remembering Amel

1 Introduction: The Anti-colonial Intellectual 3
Hicham Safieddine

2 Biographical Note: The Martyr Intellectual 10
Hicham Safieddine

PART 2
Selected Writings

3 Colonialism and Underdevelopment I: An Attempt to Understand the Colonial Relation 15

4 Colonialism and Underdevelopment II: On the Colonial Mode of Production 48

5 On the Sectarian State 84

6 Marx in the Orientalism of Edward Said 99

7 The Islamised Bourgeois Trend 111

8 The Problem of Cultural Heritage 120

List of Amel's Published Books 127
Bibliography 129
Index 131

Foreword

Ask anyone familiar with Marxism in the Arab world to mention one major Arab Marxist thinker and they will most likely – say, eight or nine times out of ten – mention one of two names: Samir Amin or Mahdi Amel. Narrow down your question to Marxist authors who have written the bulk of their work in Arabic, and Mahdi Amel will probably come first in a similar proportion. Mahdi Amel, Hassan Hamdan's pen name, was one of those intellectuals for whom revolutionary theory could not be disconnected from revolutionary practice and who remained undeterred from their effective commitment to their political convictions by the risk of being murdered.

Assassination by right-wing thugs is certainly the ultimate badge of honour for figures of the workers' movement – think of Jean Jaurès or Rosa Luxemburg – but its reverberation is naturally proportional to the fame they did achieve prior to their killing. Long before his assassination on 18 May 1987, aged 51, Mahdi Amel had stood as a towering figure in the Arab intellectual field and its Marxist subfield. He became the most prestigious intellectual figure of the renaissance of the Lebanese Communist Party (LCP) – a renaissance that started in 1968, after years of decline and ossification. During 15 years thereafter – a period that included the first half of Lebanon's long civil war (1975–90), and the party's key role in the fight against Syrian troops' intervention in 1976 on behalf of the Lebanese right-wing forces, as well as against Israeli invasions in 1978 and 1982, the LCP reached a peak in membership, with over 15,000 members in a country of four million inhabitants at that time.

Shedding its Stalinist straitjacket, the LCP shifted after 1968 into one of the most open and liveliest of the communist parties that maintained close links with the Soviet Union. This enabled it to acquire a new social and political dynamism and insert itself in the regional struggle of which the Palestine Liberation Organisation (PLO) had become the spearhead following the June 1967 Arab-Israeli war. The LCP played a major role within the Lebanese National Movement, a key protagonist of the first years of the civil war in alliance with the PLO. After the invasion by the Israeli army of one half of Lebanon in 1982, the party was the first to wage and organise an underground armed resistance to the occupation.

It is during the LCP's heyday, starting from 1973 when his first major work came out, that Mahdi Amel became the party's intellectual star. Reviving a tradition of revolutionary Marxism long stifled by the prevalence of mummified Soviet Marxism, his original and innovative Marxist thinking befitted the LCP's aggiornamento and illustrated its new intellectual pluralism. However, his thinking remained on the whole qualitatively more radical than the official line of his party, to whose central committee he was elected only shortly prior to his death.

The 1982 Israeli invasion of Lebanon represented a crucial turning point in the LCP's history. Whereas the Palestinian movement was the primary target of the occupation, the party was its main Lebanese target. In all the areas that fell under their control, Israeli occupation forces searched the party's offices, seized its weapons, and sought to arrest its prominent members. Another consequence of the invasion that was to heavily affect the LCP was the emergence of a religious Shiite current backed by the Islamic Republic of Iran, which led to the official proclamation of Hezbollah in 1985.

Hezbollah set up an Islamic Resistance as a competitor to the National Resistance Front founded by the LCP. It sought to impose its monopoly on the resistance and infuse it with a Shiite sectarian identity in order to expand its hegemony among Lebanese Shiite populations. Hezbollah had two main competitors in this regard. The first was another sectarian Shiite organisation, Amal, from which its initial nucleus had originally split. A modus vivendi was eventually reached between the two movements under the aegis of the Syrian regime, Amal's key sponsor. The second competitor was the LCP: the party had indeed a major presence among Southern Lebanon's Shiites, who constituted an important proportion of its membership.

The two most prestigious and best-known LCP members originating from Southern Lebanon were better known as intellectuals than as party leaders. The first, Hussein Mroueh, born in 1910 according to the official record, had been sent by his family as a teenager to Najaf, in Iraq, to be schooled in Islamic theology. This religious background will enable him decades later, in 1978, to publish a voluminous study of the materialist currents in Arabic Islamic philosophy, which has not been translated yet into a European language. Mroueh was assassinated on 17 February 1987.

The second high-profile LCP member from Southern Lebanon was Hassan Hamdan. Born in a communist environment, Hamdan was no less attached to his provincial roots, as revealed by his choice of pen name in which Amel refers both to his home region of Southern Lebanon (traditionally called Mount Amel) and to the figure of the 'worker' (Amel in Arabic) that is naturally dear to a Marxist. Mahdi refers to an eschatological figure in Islamic theology with a particular significance in Shiism (Mahdi means 'the guided one' in Arabic). Mahdi Amel was assassinated on 18 May 1987, three months after delivering the eulogy at Mroueh's funeral.

Hamdan's companion for close to thirty years, Evelyne Brun, whom he first met in Lyon, in France, where they were both students, passed away in Beirut on 11 May 2020. She had published two years earlier a poignant memoir of her husband titled *L'Homme aux sandales de feu* (Beirut: Al-Farabi, 2018). The book, whose title means *The Man with Sandals of Fire*, came out in a bilingual edition intertwining the French original text and its Arabic translation in a symbolic reference to the close intertwining of Hassan's and Evelyne's lives and cultures. It alternates sections directly addressing Hassan in the second person with sections speaking of him in the third person.

Evelyne's depiction of the immediate background to Mahdi Amel's assassination gives a powerful idea of our thinker's outstanding personality:

> You get back home on this April evening with a periodical in your hand. You hand it to me: 'Here is my death sentence!'. And you laugh, you laugh, of a laughter that is at once feverish, electric, but also full of delight. It is *Al Ahed*, Hezbollah's weekly publication. You point your finger at the conclusion of a specific article: 'The man who pronounced the eulogy at Hussein Mroueh's funeral in Damascus, this man will soon see that his turn has come' …
>
> [18 May] It is one of Beirut streets: Algiers Street. The death machine of fanatical hatred is getting ready. A car has been stationed every day opposite our house for a few days. Noticed by everyone in the neighbourhood, the white BMW is waiting. Algiers Street: you are now getting close. It is 10.05 am. It is here at this very moment that the tragic murder will be perpetrated … A man wearing a balaclava emerges and approaches you: 'Dr Hassan Hamdan?'. You turn around, see the pistol in his raised hand, and seize the hand brutally. Another man jumps out of the BMW and shoots you with a silenced gun in the head, chest, and belly. You fall on the ground in an effusion of blood. The car, with its three masked occupants, races away. You, the undefeated, have seen with your wide-open eyes the death come to take you. In a last act of struggle, you countered it with the resistance of life.

Evelyne Brun Hamdan had been waiting eagerly for this book to come out. She was so glad at the prospect that, at long last, English-language readers would be able to acquaint themselves with a selection of Mahdi Amel's writings. She made everything she could to speed up its publication. Sadly, she did not live long enough to hold this book in her hands. This foreword is therefore dedicated to her, for she will remain forever associated with the memory of 'the man with sandals of fire'.

Gilbert Achcar

Acknowledgements

In the wake of Mahdi Amel's assassination in 1987, his family and friends set up the Mahdi Amel Cultural Center (MACC) to preserve and disseminate his intellectual heritage in all languages. Special thanks go to the MACC's Redha Hamdan and the late Evelyne Hamdan for their leading efforts to make Amel's work available in English. Thanks also go to Alexandre Ammar, who drew on his intimate knowledge of Amel's works to help select significant texts for translation. The idea of publishing an English translation was rekindled in 2014 thanks to the enthusiastic suggestion by Vijay Prashad, Executive Director of Tricontinental Institute for Social Research and Chief Editor of LeftWord Books.

Turning the project into a reality prompted me as editor to secure two more essential ingredients whose absence had consistently stood in the way of its implementation: a qualified translator and adequate funds. Translating Amel was no easy task. Angela Giordani's excellent command of Arabic and English, her familiarity with Arab intellectual history, and her shared belief in the cultural significance and political worth of this project made for an ideal choice of translator. It was a pleasure working with her over many days and nights to fine-tune and edit the translation. We appreciate the efforts of Gilbert Achcar, Professor of Development Studies and International Relations at SOAS, who suggested helpful edits and recommended translations of key Marxist concepts. Our thanks also go to Sintia Issa for her feedback on translation excerpts and to Brill's editorial team for seeing the manuscript through to its final print version.

Procuring funds proved equally challenging in light of the dearth of concrete support for reviving the Arab Marxist tradition. Dania Dandashly's proactive fundraising efforts, on top of her own financial contribution, were a much-welcome intervention. The bulk of funding was generously provided by Mahmoud Dandashly. Both contributions reflect Dania's and Mahmoud's sincere commitment to Arab communist heritage in particular and to secular and progressive political values in general. It is a good reminder of the significance of, and need for, such goodwill at a time when these values are under assault in the Arab world by domestic and foreign reactionary forces alike.

I am fortunate to have overseen the first English translation and publication of selected writings by Amel. My only regret is that the late Evelyne, Mahdi's lifelong companion, passed away before this work saw the light. It is my hope that this volume will serve as a reminder that intellectual influence, and consequently the drive for translation, must not be unidirectional – from English to Arabic, but also from Arabic to English. May the launch of this book, whatever its shortcomings, offer a concrete incentive to take up the task of translating the rest of Amel's works as well as the works of other Arab Marxists, so that their revolutionary ideas remain alight.

Hicham Safieddine

Note on Translation

Hicham Safieddine and Angela Giordani

Amel penned part one of his essay 'Colonialism and Underdevelopment' in French. When he presented it to *al-Tariq*'s editor Mohammad Dakroub, the latter implored him to submit an Arabic version. Amel returned with an Arabic copy that impressed Dakroub.[1] From then on, all of Amel's major works were written and published in Arabic. In this translated collection, we have striven to preserve the concise yet dense Arabic writing style of Amel while seeking to maintain sentence flow and idiomatic soundness. Any apparent opaqueness must not deter readers from delving deeper, no more than similar shortcomings of European philosophy stand in the way of trying to make sense of it.

Some of Amel's arguments can be drawn out or repetitive, which may be a reflection of Amel's consciously didactic approach to analytical reasoning. But others open up new heuristic horizons. Amel was meticulous in his choice of vocabulary and innovative in his derivation of Arabic terminology intended to reflect the theoretically rich nature of his arguments. We have tried to reflect this in the translation. Frequently employed concepts which have a clear equivalence in the Hegelian, Marxian, or Islamic philosophical traditions were often rendered in their English equivalent. These include the roots and derivatives of terms like differentiation (*tafaruq*), identification (*tamathul*), determination (*tahaddud*), universality (*kawniyya*), particularity (*tamayyuz*), development or evolution (*tatawwur*), unity (*wihda*), domination (*saytara*), hegemony (*haymana*), overexploitation (*fa'id al-istighlal*), financial oligarchy (*tughma maliyya*), principal contradiction (*tanaqud ra'isi*), antagonistic contradiction (*tanaqud tanahuri*), cultural heritage (*al-turath*), Islamic law (*shari'a*), and Islamic jurisprudence (*fiqh*).

Other concepts had more than one possible equivalent, and were therefore trickier to translate. The concept of *takhalluf* could be translated as 'underdevelopment' or 'backwardness'. Both terms were in common usage during Amel's time in anti-colonial literature. Given the preponderance of 'underdevelopment' today and the negative association of 'backwardness', we opted for the former in most cases, particularly in reference to political economy, and the latter only in relation to questions of culture. The concept of *tawazun haymani* was generally rendered hegemonic 'balance' rather than 'equilibrium'.

---

1 See Hamdan 2018, p. 437.

We were less strict in translating the concept of *bunya ijtimaʿiyya*, using either 'social structure' (for the most part), or 'social formation'. In line with contemporary terminology, we translated *al-insan* (human) as man. Still other concepts were much more tied to the colonial context, rendering their translation far from straightforward. This applied to certain fundamental features of the Colonial Mode of Production (CoMP) like dead-locked contradiction (*tanaqud maʾziqi*) and crisis-ridden contradiction (*tanaqud azami*). Other CoMP-related concepts have an equivalent in dependency or world systems theory parlance, but they do not fully capture Amel's articulation. A primary example is *al-burjwaziyya al-istiʿmariyya*, which we translated as 'colonialist bourgeoisie'. The more conventional translation would have been the 'metropolitan bourgeoisie'. We could have also used "imperialist bourgeoisie". Our reasoning was as follows: Firstly, Amel could have used the transliterated form (metroboliyya) since he makes reference once to the word in its transliterated form. He also uses other transliterated concepts like 'imbiryaliyya' to denote 'imperialism' and 'kulunyaliyya' to denote 'colonial'. Secondly, Amel generally avoided terms like core and periphery which privilege the social reality of capitalist countries, by placing them at the core, over that of their colonised counterparts, and metropole can carry such a signification. Lastly, 'colonialist bourgeoisie' is used in the translation of Frantz Fanon's canonical anti-colonial text, which sets a precedent. By opting for the less common usage, we might have steered clear of conventional usage in dependency theory literature, but we believe that we have stayed closer to the course of Amel's own conceptual universe. A less challenging but highly significant choice of translation was the distinction between nationalist (*qawmi*) and national (*watani*). While the difference is not always significant in English, it is highly so in the context of national liberation movements. The national (as opposed to nationalist) struggle denoted the anti-colonial form of class struggle and thereby has a very progressive connotation in Arabic compared to a nationalist struggle. With rare exceptions, we dropped the transliterated term so as not to interrupt flow.

Overall, we have tried to be as truthful to the original meaning in terms of both text and context while remaining attentive to readership expectations. We did so knowing that translation is not always possible, let alone perfect.

PART 1

Remembering Amel

∵

CHAPTER 1

Introduction: The Anti-colonial Intellectual

Hicham Safieddine

In the mid-twentieth century, national liberation movements fought fiercely against European colonialism and American imperialism. The ideological field of struggle was a highly active front in this battle. As more "Third World" countries gained formal political independence but remained subjugated economically, their Marxist-leaning intellectuals articulated theories of 'underdevelopment' that challenged liberal notions of modernisation on the one hand and Eurocentric articulations of anti-imperialism on the other.[1]

This translation of selected writings is an attempt to shed light on the notable contribution in this field of Arab Marxist Mahdi Amel. Amel (1936–87) was a prominent theoretician of colonialism and 'underdevelopment' in an Arab context and a long-time Lebanese Communist Party member during the era of national liberation. He also wrote on a wide range of subjects that are highly pertinent to current debates about the Arab region. They included sectarianism, political Islam, orientalism, culture and revolution, and the relationship of cultural heritage to modernity – all of which he explored through the lens of class analysis. He hailed from the Marxist-Leninist tradition and was influenced, in an undogmatic manner, by Althusser's school of thought. But above all else, he was an anti-colonial Marxist. Throughout his writings, he sought to produce a theory of Marxism that took colonial rather than capitalist social reality as its starting point. He explained underdevelopment according to colonial reality's *own* terms. He avoided terms like periphery or Third World, which decentred or hierarchised this reality, even if implicitly. He equally insisted on using concepts like liberation, which affirmed active and future-oriented resistance on the part of the colonised, rather than decolonisation, which conjured up a passive process of illusory return to some pre-colonial past.

---

1 Half a century later, their contribution to the evolution of Marxist theory is often relegated to the margins of Anglophone debates on political economy. When broached, their works tend to be summarily grouped under the rubric of dependency theory associated with a handful of authors. These authors include Fernando Cardoso and Andre Gunder Frank in Latin America, Hamza Alvi in South Asia, and Samir Amin in the Arab world. Until recently, Marx's own treatment of the colonial world has been largely ignored or reductively associated with certain concepts like the Asiatic mode of production. For a more substantial treatment, see Anderson 2010.

 | DOI:10.1163/9789004444249_002

Amel's centring of the colonial experience was manifest in his analytical treatment of the colonial relation. In Amel's theoretical universe, colonialism itself is the *objective basis* for the unity of the colonised country's social formation. It constitutes the historical framework for the development of the forces of production in colonial societies. It is an all-encompassing, rather than purely economic, relationship within which a fusion took place between the capitalist and pre-capitalist modes of production. This fusion gave rise to a new relationship of structural dependency. 'All of my inquiry', Amel wrote, 'is an attempt to define this form of dependency, and it has yielded the concept of the colonial mode of production (CoMP)'.[2]

The CoMP is 'the form of capitalism structurally dependent on imperialism in its historical formation and contemporary development'.[3] Contradictions that shape and drive class struggle under a CoMP operate at the level of the interaction of the two interdependent structures of capitalist and colonised social formations. This creates multiple and complex layers of contradictions.[4]

Amel set out to discern the characteristics that distinguished the CoMP from the capitalist mode of production. In the process, he produced a lexicon of terms and concepts specific to the CoMP. What might appear as conceptual shortcomings for classical Marxist thought, Amel saw as theoretical affirmations of the particularity of the colonial social formation. The CoMP, for instance, was defined by the very fact that it was prevented from developing into a full mode of production. Political instability, often cited as evidence of weak state formation or ascribed to a defective political culture, was itself a feature of the phenomenon of class substitution – rather than class revolution – prevalent under the colonial mode of production and expressed in the form of frequent military coups or short-lived governments. This instability, Amel pointed out, is partly a consequence of the stability, not stagnancy, of the overall social structure as a result of the blocking of social development under the CoMP. 'Class substitution occurs within the bounds of the social structure itself without bringing about a structural change in the social mode of production'.[5] At the centre of class substitution under a CoMP are the petite bourgeoisie. Whereas this faction of the bourgeoisie is conceptualised by Amel as marginal

2 See Amel 2013, p. 524.

3 See Amel 1990, p. 11.

4 As Amel notes, 'There is the basic contradiction that encompasses the structural contradictions in each particular structure; then there is the complication presented by the existence of a dominant structure in the unity; and finally there is a dominant contradiction, which is the primary contradiction, in the unity of contradictions in each structure'. Amel 2013, p. 529.

5 Amel 2013, p. 542.

and 'parasitic' in the capitalist mode of production that evolved in Europe, it is nothing less than the 'centre-point of history's movement' in a colonial formation.

Another feature of CoMP is the relative lack of class differentiation. This is not a sign of underdeveloped capitalist relations, but a structural limitation of CoMP. Class struggle therefore involves the struggle for the exploited classes' very existence as a class, 'i.e. as a struggle to free up the historical process of its own class formation. Herein lies the distinction of the [class] contradiction in colonial society'. The relation of exploitation is indirect, with the principal class enemy being the colonial structure itself as opposed to a particular class. As a result, the form of class struggle in colonial society differs from the conventional form of the proletarian revolution in capitalist Europe. In colonial societies, the socialist revolution is inseparable from national liberation:

> The struggle for national liberation is the *sole* historical form that distinguishes class struggle in the colonial [structural] formation. Whoever misses this essential point in the movement of our modern history and attempts to substitute class struggle with 'nationalist struggle' or reduces the national struggle to a purely economic struggle loses the ability to understand our historical reality and thus also [the ability] to control its transformation.[6]

The transition to socialism – for capitalist and colonised societies alike – necessitates the severing of this colonial relation: 'The revolution against colonialism is the only path to liberate human history.'

In 1968, Amel set out his line of thinking about the relation between colonialism and underdevelopment in a pioneering study titled 'Colonialism and Underdevelopment'. It was published as a two-part series in *al-Tariq*, the Lebanese Communist Party's political and intellectual journal. Both essays are translated in this anthology in full.[7] They are titled respectively: 'An Attempt to Understand the Colonial Relationship' and 'The Colonial Mode of Production'. Amel would later develop his ideas into a more in-depth theorisation of the CoMP in his magnum opus titled *Theoretical Prolegomena to the Study of the Impact of Socialist Thought on the National Liberation Movement*. In 1972, Amel

6 Amel 2013, p. 472.

7 Editor's note: The original Arabic text of part two includes an introductory section that mostly sums up part one of Amel's study *On Colonialism and Underdevelopment*. Given that the first part was translated in full, the introductory section was dropped from this translation of part two.

published the first two parts of this work, 'On Contradiction' and 'On the Colonial Mode of Production'. The third part, titled 'On the Staging of History', was put on hold. At that time, the rise of neoliberalism worldwide was accompanied in the post-Nasserist Arab world by the spread of conservative ideological currents, including a culturalist turn. This reoriented Amel's intellectual output towards what he saw as pressing problems facing Arab nationalism. In response to a Kuwait conference held in April 1974 to discuss the purported crisis of civilisational development in the Arab world, Amel lambasted the Arab national bourgeoisies for turning their own crisis of rule into a crisis of Arab civilisation as such.[8] He argued that the idea – upheld by many liberals – that Arabo-Islamic 'cultural heritage' (*turath*) was potentially incompatible with modernity was itself a problem of the present, i.e. a problem of how these thinkers interpreted the past, not a problem of the past. Heritage itself was conjured up by imperialist forces in an orientalist manner that justified the latter's 'civilising mission', which to Amel's dismay was scandalously internalised by the bourgeois leadership of several national movements.[9]

Amel was also critical of Edward Said's portrayal of Marx's thought. Like other Marxists, Amel argued that Said, in his influential book *Orientalism*, fails to properly contextualise the selective passages of Marx he cites and, more significantly, treats all Western thought as a monolith without reference to its class character. This is because Said ignores the materialist basis on which Marx's thought rests and thereby denies its revolutionary novelty. Amel found it equally necessary to counter the rise of anti-intellectual 'everyday thought' in the press. In a manuscript, posthumously published and titled *A Critique of Everyday Thought*, he identified three major categories of quotidian thought: nihilist, obscurantist, and Islamised bourgeois.

These emerging trends signalled ideological shifts in Arab bourgeois thought that took place as a result of two developments. The first was the liberal turn of certain nationalist forces in the post-Nasserist era. The second was the rise of Islam as a force in Arab politics following the Islamic revolution in Iran and the expansion of Saudi Salafism. In his critique of Islamised bourgeois thought, Amel steered clear of culturalist and idealist interpretations. For Amel, Islam's revolutionary or reactionary character must be measured in relation to its class rather than metaphysical character: 'Anyone who speaks about political Islam in a general sense without defining the particular class character of its political being – whether revolutionary or anti-revolutionary, reactionary bourgeois

---

8 On Amel as one of the few intellectuals to resist the culturalist trend in explaining Arab social ills, see Massad 2007, p. 20.

9 Amel expressed these views in *A Crisis of Arab Civilization or a Crisis of the Arab Bourgeoisies?* (Amel 2002).

or anti-bourgeois – is speaking from a dominant bourgeois position'.[10] Under Amel's framework, the primary contradiction in Islam is not between belief and atheism, but between those who defer to power and those who defy it. It follows that institutionalised Islam of the ruling classes, including that of Andalusian rationalist philosopher Ibn Rushd, was often a hindrance to revolutionary change.[11]

The Lebanese civil war, which broke out in 1975, was another major development that influenced Amel's intellectual output. Amel examined the causes of the war and analysed sectarianism through the prism of class analysis. He is arguably the first Lebanese thinker to identify sectarianism as a strictly modern and political rather than a primordial and religious phenomenon. Amel elucidates the contradictions and crises of the Lebanese state as a simultaneously bourgeois and sectarian system of rule. Sects, Amel asserts, are not, as bourgeois thought would have it, stand-alone social formations. A sect is a determined political relation embedded in a particular political system, sectarianism. Put differently, a sect is a historically determined form of class domination particular to CoMP. The book was equally a criticism of a strand of leftist thought that fell into the trap of implicitly reproducing or confirming Lebanese bourgeois thought by granting sects an ontological existence independent of political relations.

Amel went further and exposed the falsehood of bourgeois tropes of power-sharing arrangements among sects. Fair political 'participation' among sects, he argued, was a utopian slogan raised by the non-hegemonic factions of the dominant bourgeoisie in order to improve their own class position within the sectarian divisions of power. Sectarian balance is only possible through the hegemony of a particular sect, not participation of all sects. When this hegemony is threatened, the fascist solution is proposed to salvage the system, as the sectarian right-wing Kataeb party attempted to do during the civil war. Amel premonitorily warned that substituting one sectarian hegemony, Maronite, with another, say Sunni or Shia, would not alter the sectarian nature and solve the crisis but simply reproduce it.[12]

Amel did not survive the Lebanese civil war. He was assassinated on 18 May 1987. His elimination was part of a killing spree by sectarian Islamist forces tar-

10 See Amel 2005, p. 330.

11 In English, Ibn Rushd is commonly referred to as Averroes.

12 Amel published three major studies on the subject: Introduction into the *Theory in Political Practice: An Inquiry into the Causes of the Lebanese Civil War* (Amel 1979); *A Gateway into Refuting Sectarian Thought: The Palestinian Cause in the Ideology of the Lebanese Bourgeoisie* (Amel 1980); and *On the Sectarian State* (Amel 1986).

geting communist intellectuals. Thirty years later, a new generation of Arab leftists that came of age during the Arab uprisings have revived his legacy in public spaces and on social media. His Arabic publications remain in print. Recent scholarly interest in the Anglophone academy has provided a preliminary peak into his thought. These studies, however, have largely remained cursory and in some cases distorted by postmodern inflections or romanticised generalisations.[13] Reading Amel in his own words is a major step towards taking full and critical stock of his thought, whatever its contradictions and evolutionary transformation. Doing so would place his thought in comparative perspective to contemporary Marxist theories of colonialism and underdevelopment, rather than provincialize his contribution or use his assassination as a tool to discredit Hezbollah today in ahistorical and decontextualized accounts of the role of communist and Islamist forces in resisting Zionism.

The current collection brings for the first time to an English audience lengthy excerpts from six major works by Amel. These include the two founding texts on colonialism and underdevelopment in which Amel began to grapple with the question of dependency, his treatise on sectarianism and the state, his critique of Edward Said's analysis of Marx, his exposure of emerging Islamised bourgeois trends of thought as part of a broader critique of everyday thought, and his reflection on cultural heritage as perceived by the Arab bourgeoisies.

With over a dozen published books to Amel's credit, this collection is a long way from introducing all aspects of his thought, including his study on the staging of history. The latter offers a valuable window into the evolution of his thinking on temporality and the determinist aspects of Louis Althusser and Étienne Balibar's structuralism in which Amel discerned implicit antirevolutionary tendencies. In this and all other writings, Amel stressed the interplay of the universal and the particular. His Marxism, like that of other anti-colonial Marxists, serves as a powerful rebuttal to persistent post-colonial polemics that reduce Marxism to a provincial theory of mere European relevance or Marxist dogma steeped in Western thought. Back in Amel's days, Marxism was a major current of political action and intellectual activity in the Arab world. Reviving this thought is crucial to understanding the historical conjuncture of national liberation in Arab history that is often dismissed as a passing moment of progressive reformation or derided as a failed project of modernisation.

13 For recent studies and writings in English that specifically address Amel's work, see Frangie 2012, pp. 465–82; Sing and Younes 2013, pp. 149–91; Abu Rabi' 2004, pp. 318–43; Tohme 2012; Prashad 2014.

Non-European Marxist thought like Amel's remains equally relevant for ongoing struggles around the world, if only as a reminder of the need to renew Marxist thought based on the concrete and particular social realities of today and the demands of existing political struggles. Amel emphasised the unifying nature of political struggle. For him, transformative rather than speculative theoretical activity, including the production of a theory of underdevelopment, was part and parcel of his political struggle. His lived experience and untimely death, briefly sketched in the following section, were as much an expression of anti-colonial struggle as were his writings. Both have yet to be fully incorporated into the legacy of national liberation thought with its triumphs and tragedies.[14]

---

14 I wish to thank Evelyne Hamdan, Redha Hamdan, and Gilbert Achcar for their helpful comments on drafts of this introduction.

CHAPTER 2

Biographical Note: The Martyr Intellectual

Hicham Safieddine

Beirut was the city of Mahdi Amel's childhood and political beginnings. He was born Hassan Hamdan in 1936 to a family that hailed from southern Lebanon, or Jabal Amel, which partly inspired his pen name. His father, Abdullah, had settled in Beirut in the wake of WWI and set up shop as a textile merchant. Amel came of age during the 1950s. This was the golden age of pan-Arabism under the leadership of Egyptian President Gamal Abdel Nasser and national liberation struggles across the globe. At school, Amel was influenced by his biology teacher Shafiq al-Hout, who later became a prominent member of the Palestine Liberation Organization. The Palestinian educator introduced Amel to Marxist literature that came to populate his modest home library. Teacher and student debated and discussed the Arab world's pressing issues of the day like the Algerian revolution and the liberation of Palestine. They also took to the streets to support these causes. Upon completing high school, the young Amel yearned to pursue higher education abroad, something his father opposed. Thanks to financial and moral support from his sisters, he set sail to Montpelier in 1956 and shortly after settled in Lyon, where he met and married his lifelong companion Evelyne Brun.[1]

In the next thirty years, Amel's life was punctuated by the ebb and flow of anti-colonial struggle. He moved from France to Algeria and back to Lebanon. While studying philosophy at the University of Lyon, Amel joined a clandestine gathering of Arab communists and mingled with fellow French communist students. He wove informal links with the Lebanese Communist Party and partook in its activities. In those formative years, he read a wide array of literature relevant to the question of colonialism and underdevelopment: Georges Balandier on Third Worldism, Hasan Riyad and Anouar Abdel Malik on Nasserism, Charles Bettelheim on underdevelopment in India, Gerard Chaliand on the Kurdish question, and Frantz Fanon, André Mandouze, and Pierre Bourdieu on Algeria.

1 We know much more about Amel's personal life thanks to the biography recently published by his wife. See Hamdan 2018. The details about his life in this note are largely based on her account.

 | DOI:10.1163/9789004444249_003

Amel was particularly drawn to the Algerian struggle for independence. The room he shared with Evelyne served as a secret meeting place for underground Algerian operatives in France and a hiding place for suitcases stuffed with cash contributions to armed militants. When Algeria gained its independence in 1962, the couple were drawn by the promise of building a socialist future in a free Algeria. They accepted an invitation by the Algerian consul in Lyon to move to the picturesque city of Kasantina. Amel taught philosophy and politics at the city's teacher's college. He simultaneously completed his doctoral dissertation under the supervision of Henri Maldiney. The dissertation made reference to the colonial mode of production, a concept he would later develop much further into a theory of underdevelopment. The optimism of these early years waned into disillusionment after Boumediene's rise to power in 1965, which Amel saw as a shift towards bureaucratised authoritarian rule. The defeat of Arab armies in the 1967 war was another tipping point. The subsequent rise of radical and pro-Palestinian leftist politics back in Lebanon offered a glimmer of hope. Amel embarked on the third and final leg of his journey. He returned to Beirut.

In Beirut, Amel taught at a high school in the southern city of Saida and later at the Lebanese University. During his early years, he delved deeper into the question of underdevelopment. He acquainted himself with the works of Carlos Romero and Gunder Frank on dependency in Latin America, Mahmoud Hussein's and Anaour Abdel Malik's on Egypt, Jean Suret-Kanal's on the Asiatic mode of production, and Poulantzas' on Fascism. He continued to deepen his grasp of Marxist theories of political economy as articulated by Rosa Luxemburg and more recent interpretations of Marx by Louis Althusser and Antonio Gramsci. He did so without neglecting emerging post-colonial writings by Michel Foucault and later Jacques Derrida. All the while, he kept abreast of local and regional news on culture, politics, and anti-colonial struggles around the world as he penned and published his own thoughts on these subjects. He also dived headlong into reforming the Lebanese Communist Party, having now officially joined it. Amel – alongside other young cadres – pushed for an agenda of national liberation that saw the struggle against Israeli aggression and the national question in general as an integral part of the struggle for socialism.

As the Lebanese civil war that broke out in 1975 grew more sectarian in character, Amel continued to warn against attempts to suppress the class character of the conflict. He opposed reactionary forces in deed as much as he did in word. During the 1982 Israeli siege and bombardment of Beirut, Amel joined the front lines of aid work and coined the defiant motto: 'you are not defeated as long as you resist'.

Throughout the war, and without fail, Amel preached revolutionary socialism in public fora and private gatherings: to his Lebanese University students, to south Lebanon's tobacco farmers, to family members, and to communist comrades who eventually elected him to the party's central committee in 1987. By then, however, the Lebanese communist and leftist forces were on the retreat as sectarian militias dominated the battle scene. Sectarian Islamist forces launched a wave of assassinations against communist intellectuals. On 17 February 1987, another stalwart of Arab Marxist thought, Hussein Muruwwa, was assassinated in cold blood in his Beirut apartment. He was 87. Amel, who was feeling increasingly isolated among his party peers, eulogised his dear friend and foresaw his own death but refused to go into hiding. Three months later, on 18 May, he was walking down Beirut's Algeria St. when an assailant gunned him down. He was 51, but his memory as a martyr intellectual of the communist movement in Lebanon lives on.

PART 2

Selected Writings

∵

CHAPTER 3

Colonialism and Underdevelopment I: An Attempt to Understand the Colonial Relation

It seems natural and necessary to speak of colonialism and underdevelopment as related phenomena.[1] We have become accustomed, in our theoretical and political work, to posit the former as a cause of the latter. The link between colonialism and underdevelopment has taken root in our minds, in fact, to a point that it no longer gives us pause. It is a problem that no longer incites serious – i.e. scientific – thought because it appears as self-evident. In its appearance as self-evident, it has disappeared as a problem. The scientific mind, however, is leery of what is self-evident and accepts it only when proven, at which point the self-evident becomes true. Scientific truth subsists in what is proven and verified, not in appearance. Insofar as it appears to be true, what appears as self-evident often distorts truth and obscures its foundation. It satisfies only lazy minds whose activity has been paralysed by fear of treading the path of truth and their need to avoid its dangers. Appearance conceals truth even if it is the manifestation of truth. Herein lies the danger and effectiveness of appearance. If we were to say, for example, that colonialism is a cause and creator of 'underdevelopment', our statement would be correct. The fact that this statement's correctness is so strikingly clear to us, however, marks the weakness in our thought; we have been dazzled, almost blinded, by the clarity of the causal link between colonialism and 'underdevelopment'.

The point, however, is not to parrot this claim. Rather, the point is to interrogate the *modalities* and structural causes of the link between these two phenomena that constitute the foundation of our society and the essence of its historical development. Designating colonialism as a cause of 'underdevelopment' is not the issue. The real problem is in specifying the kind of causality that links underdevelopment to colonialism. Documenting reality as it appears to us does not solve this problem. To glean the essence and structure of reality, we must dispel appearances and transcend them. This requires that we devise theoretical tools which alone are capable of producing scientific knowledge

1 This study was first published in *al-Tariq* magazine, no. 8, 1968. Editor's note: The translation is based on a reproduction of the study as an appended text to the 2013 edition of Amel's *Theoretical Prolegomena for the Study of the Impact of Socialist Thought on the National Liberation Movement*, first published in 1972.

 | DOI:10.1163/9789004444249_004

of unfolding reality. These theoretical tools are called concepts, and they are the product of theoretical thinking. If we want to understand 'underdevelopment' scientifically, we must first come up with the theoretical tools required for such an understanding. To be precise, what we want to emphasise at the outset of this study is that we cannot understand 'underdevelopment', which is our present historical reality, unless we formulate a theory of it. This scientific theory cannot be other than Marxist. It is a foundational premise of our research that Marxist thought alone is capable of giving us a theory of this all-encompassing phenomenon [of underdevelopment].

It might be said that there is something of 'demagoguery' in the above statement that conflicts with scientific thought. Despite our belief that our argument is true, we do not present it as established truth, but, rather, as a hypothesis that will be true only when proven. Put more precisely, the above outlines a method of thinking that must prove its correctness by producing theoretical knowledge of 'underdevelopment'.

We have said that Marxism is the only thought that can make sense of the phenomenon of 'underdevelopment'. This claim is not the outcome of some formal process of reasoning. It is based on the very emergence of Marxism and its development [as a theory] through the examination of the complex phenomena of 'underdevelopment' and imperialism. The birth of Marxist thought among us, or, more precisely, the birth of *our* Marxist thought, can only happen through the process of addressing this historical phenomenon. This [process] is a principal condition, even an absolute necessity, for bringing about the birth [of this thought]. This is because the process of understanding 'underdevelopment' is one and the same as the process of the birth of our Marxist thought. This is not just one of the most important theoretical issues facing us, but the most important issue obstructing Marxism's development among us. We therefore saw it as necessary to begin this study with some methodological remarks.

If we want to liberate our thought and make it creative, or, in other words, capable of producing scientific knowledge, we must undertake what might be called a *methodological revolution*. Method refers to the modality by which the thought process takes reality as its subject. We have become accustomed to analysing reality, our [colonial] reality, by applying pre-formed Marxist thought. We tend to apply this thought in a way that fits our reality while simultaneously preserving this pre-formed thought that we have adopted. The difficulty in this approach lay in the attempt to reconcile our belief in this thought and its accordance with reality, i.e. in the attempt to gain scientific knowledge of reality. We have so far attempted to solve this problem through [developing] an applied theory.

If we look closely at this applied method, however, we will see that the starting point in its treatment of reality is in fact pre-formed thought, not reality in its fullness and complexity. Herein lies our first methodological error: The application of pre-formed thought to a new reality cannot in the end produce theoretical conceptualisation, i.e. knowledge, of this reality. Rather, this application is the violent insertion of this reality into the fixed moulds of pre-formed thought. It casts [our] new historical reality into the moulds of this pre-formed thought so that reality conforms to pre-formed thought. As a result, what is new in this reality has been lost [on us], and we have produced ignorance rather than knowledge. Our method of reasoning has resulted in the opposite of what we wanted: it has demonstrated [Marxist] thought's inability to comprehend our historical reality. This is not, in fact, the case. The failure to understand our historical reality is not a failure of Marxist thought, but, rather, a failure of [our] applied theory to comprehend both this reality and [Marxist] thought. Such a theoretical application is in essence at once idealist and empiricist: idealist in its assumption of conformity between thought and reality, and empirical in its assumption of reality's resemblance across temporal and spatial boundaries and their differentiation. Such an applied theory departs and differs widely from practical and theoretical Marxist methodology. If we truly want to establish sound Marxist thinking by and for us that is capable of perceiving reality scientifically, we must not begin with Marxism as a pre-formed system of thought that we attempt to apply to our reality. Instead, we must begin with our reality in its own process of formation. As such, we would be engaging in a process of thinking about this particular historical reality that never hesitates to take the bases of our pre-formed thought as an object of *methodological* inquiry in order to shape it in a Marxist manner. Taking our pre-formed Marxist thought as an object of inquiry is the only way to enable the formation of our own Marxist thought.

We must clarify here a point that might be ambiguous: This critique of pre-formed thought is not to be undertaken in the name of either some other thought opposed to it or a return to our so-called authentic thought. It is to be done in the name of Marxism itself. Marxism is the only kind of thought that is capable of carrying out fearless self-criticism. This is because self-critique constitutes the momentum of [Marxism's] development and vitality; indeed, it is the primary form of its development. On the other hand, we must note that this process of critique is not a formal move, but the very process of theoretically understanding our historical reality.

If we were to grasp this method and its new point of departure (from reality to thought in a critique of pre-formed thought that is [a process] of building thought-in-formation), this would remove our fear of resorting specifically to Marx in attempting to understand colonialism and 'underdevelopment'. This is so even if our taking recourse to Marx appears contradictory to our method.

No matter what, this contradiction happens because, on the one hand, we cannot understand Marx, with whom our attempt to understand 'underdevelopment' begins, except through 'underdeveloped' reality. On the other hand, we cannot understand this 'underdeveloped' reality except through Marxist thought. In other words, understanding Marx, as a starting point for our thought, can only happen through understanding the reality of 'underdevelopment', and understanding the latter cannot happen without understanding the former. The existence of the former supposes the existence of the latter, and vice versa. It looks like a vicious circle. It is not a formal but a dialectical contradiction. Its evolution, moreover, is nothing but the process of struggle to produce a Marxist theory of 'underdevelopment', that is to find a theoretical-practical solution to 'underdevelopment'. The contradiction between this thought and this reality – the relation between them – is real, not logical. It is the driving force in the process of producing Marxism for 'underdevelopment', i.e. in the process of the birth of our Marxist thought.

We will not expound more on this methodological point, despite its importance. Let us return to the starting point of our study and lay the ground as to why it should be accepted.

As previously stated, the new aspect of our method is its point of departure in reality rather than pre-formed thought. It is worth noting here that our point of departure is also Marx's point of departure. We do not seek similarity or emulation in this regard. At its base, Marx's thought was formed through a critical inspection of the capitalist system of production.[2] At a basic level, [Marx's thought] is Western thought that attempted to understand – in the course of its construction into a well-developed theory – a specific historical reality, namely Western capitalist reality. In other words, we can say that Marx's thought and the main Marxist conceptual apparatus are, without doubt, a direct outcome of a specifically Western historical experience.

We should note here that the historical particularity of the emergence of Marxist thought and the formation of its primary foundations does not at all negate its universality as potential thought and actual reality. The universality of Marxist thought lies in the fact that it is a scientific analysis of a determined

2 Editor's note: Amel uses the phrase *nizam al-intaj* (system of production) throughout this first part of his *al-Tariq* essay and switches to *namat al-intaj* (mode of production) in the second part.

historical phenomenon that is particular to the West: capitalism. Universality – as it exists – is always particular, and particularity is the basic condition of the existence of universality. This is one of Marxism's most, if not the most, important theoretical maxims. By understanding Marx's thought in this manner, and by specifying its historical emergence and formation, we are submitting it to [analysis guided by] one of [his thought's] most fundamental theoretical principles, one that necessarily forces us to refuse any attempt to apply his [preformed] thought to our reality. As we have said, the attempt at application inevitably leads to a failed understanding of [this thought] and our reality. It is an attempt rooted in ignorance and denial of the very Marxist premise to which we just alluded: universality's particularity. In submitting Marxist thought to Marxist principles, our method is purely Marxist, and we did not arrive at this methodological necessity except through our attempt at a historicist analysis of the phenomenon of 'underdevelopment'.

We must further note that this methodological necessity appears as if it precedes the theoretical process of understanding 'underdevelopment', even though it is in fact a necessary product of this process. Stated otherwise, if submitting Marx's thought to a critique of the historical reality of 'underdevelopment' is a basic condition for producing Marxist thought capable of understanding this reality, then this condition, even if it logically precedes the process of knowing 'underdevelopment', is actually produced through the process of this knowing. We are still unaware of this methodological necessity because we have not yet become aware of the *practical* value of the necessity of theoretical knowledge of 'underdevelopment'. Our lack of such awareness has its own major historical significance. The main reason for failing to produce a Marxist theory of 'underdevelopment' can be traced first and foremost to the fact that we have not yet realised – in our political work, by which I mean our struggles against 'underdevelopment' or, more precisely, our class struggle within the framework of 'underdevelopment' – the necessity of this theory. Our political work, i.e. our class struggle, has not imposed upon us the necessity of producing this theory. This phenomenon must clarify the form of our political work, i.e. the form of existence of class struggle [in our society]. It should also push us to admit to ourselves in a scientific manner divorced from demagogic optimism – because scientific truth alone is the sole source of true optimism – that our political work has not attained this theoretical knowledge. Put more precisely, our 'political' [sic] work must become political, and bounded by 'underdevelopment'. This designation of our political work as apolitical directly reflects our particular class reality. We may therefore say that the absence of a Marxist theory of 'underdevelopment' is in and of itself a primary manifestation of the phenomena of 'underdevelopment'. We cannot understand this manifestation without understanding the phenomenon of 'underdevelopment' [that produced it].

We thus return to our initial starting point: Scientific analysis of the phenomenon of 'underdevelopment' must be regarded as an attempt to form Marxist theory determined as a critique of 'underdevelopment'. If knowledge of 'underdevelopment' is a critique of Marxist pre-formed thought, then critique of this thought is the production of Marxist theory in a process of formation and universalisation. This takes place through a critique of, which is also a revolt against, 'underdevelopment'. The process of producing Marxist thought as critique of 'underdevelopment' is therefore first and foremost a revolutionary rather than theorising process. Stated more precisely, the revolutionary process is a single contradictory movement established on two main, distinct levels: practical and theoretical, each of which determines the other in its defined role within the single movement. The structural link between these two levels ensures that theoretical activity will be something far from abstract metaphysical speculation, as [this link] directs every action towards the revolutionary objective of transforming reality. In its structure, basis, and objective, theoretical activity is thus revolutionary praxis so long as it is not separated from the overarching revolutionary movement to transform reality. Theoretical activity loses its revolutionary quality and becomes speculation if it is separated from this revolutionary movement, if its goal is no longer the transformation of reality. The process of producing a theory of 'underdevelopment' is therefore revolutionary, because this theory is determined as a theory of revolutionary action, i.e. as a theory of revolution against 'underdevelopment' within the historical movement of the structural evolution of 'underdevelopment'.

The production of a theory of 'underdevelopment' as part of our critique of Marxist thought, i.e. as part of our revolutionary action – itself a particular class struggle – is the very essence of producing our Marxist thought. Theoretical thought is constructed as part of the movement of revolutionary transformation of reality rather than in isolation from this movement and this reality. The structure of theoretical thought must reflect the structure of the historical field in which it was built. It is therefore possible for there to be a difference between Marxist thought under our consideration and Marx's own thought, even though they are part of a single intellectual unity. This difference is not necessarily a contradiction or mutual negation. Rather, it is the only form taken by this unity's comprehensive and universal existence as a determined historical unity.

Having concluded these quick methodological remarks, which we saw to be necessary, we will now turn to treating our problem. In this attempt of ours, we must have the right to err before stating what is right.

∵

If we truly wanted to understand the phenomenon of 'underdevelopment', our inquiry must commence with the colonial relation, approaching it as a fundamental, productive relation between two different systems of production. In other words, we must approach it as a relation of domination between two kinds of countries with different social structures. A theoretical determination of the colonial relation and its historical development is a basic condition for theoretically defining 'underdevelopment'. The link between colonialism and 'underdevelopment' is not only chronological, but, first and foremost, structural. Emphasising chronology while neglecting structure leads to a false understanding of [colonialism and 'underdevelopment'] that separates and externalises one from the other, which makes it impossible to understand the causal relationship between the two phenomena, unless we want to understand causality only in a mechanistic, empirical way that distances us from the historical reality at hand: Colonialism is not a cause of underdevelopment because the former precedes the latter. Colonialism is a cause of underdevelopment because of the structural relation between them by which colonialism causes underdevelopment, producing the latter continuously in the movement of colonialism's specific becoming. The difficulty does not lie in emphasising the existence of a structural link between these two phenomena, but in defining the form of this link in a scientific manner, namely in defining the specific kind of causality linking colonialism to 'underdevelopment'.

If understanding the colonial relation is a condition for understanding underdevelopment, we must begin with Marx. This is because his writings, especially *Capital*, contain valuable insights that may help us in treating our problem.

Here we should pause to note the significance of the way we read Marx. Marx does not treat colonialism as a problem in and of itself. Rather, he addresses it incidentally, [namely] as a necessary [step] in his study of capitalism. Marx's major theoretical concern is to define the scientific laws of capitalism's historical development. He does not deal with colonialism except to clarify some aspects of capitalism's development. Marx, in other words, examines colonialism from the perspective of capitalism. We, on the other hand, must treat the problem from an entirely different perspective, namely that of colonialism, not capitalism. Our theoretical progression in this problem is thus the inverse of Marx's theoretical progression. We do not depend on Marx in this inquiry of ours, nor, as a result, do we set out to discuss capitalism unless doing so helps us understand colonialism and 'underdevelopment'. The line of our thought in its various dimensions must therefore intersect with Marx's line of thought, and there must be a meeting point between these two lines. Indeed, the direction of inquiry is different because it is aimed at a different reality. While colonialism is a single reality, it differs according to its historical existence. In a colonised 'underdeveloped' country, [the reality of colonialism] is different than it is in a capitalist, colonising country. This difference in the reality of colonialism necessarily produces difference in how we view it. This is why it is not only possible for us to differ with Marx on the problem of colonialism, but necessary if our thought process is scientifically precise.[3]

Marx, and Lenin after him, consider colonialism in general to be a historical necessity of capitalism's own development. Indeed, Marx views colonialism, so to speak, as a simultaneously logical and historical necessity. What is meant by this is that capitalism, in the process of its historical development, necessarily tends towards infinite expansion, either by way of establishing direct imperialist rule in countries beyond its realm, or by way of the foreign market as a global market for capitalism. This expansionist tendency is inherent to the process of [capitalism's] becoming. The failure to appropriately actualise this necessity in some circumstances does not by any means negate the fact of its existence. Rather, it expressly clarifies how the development of capitalism in such circumstances is incapable of actualising this logical, real necessity, as was the case in Germany. Herein lies the primary cause of imperialist wars.

Marx specifies the reasons that necessarily pushed capitalism towards its colonial development. He does not, however, specify for us the causes for this

3 It might be said: You rely on Marx and forget Lenin, even though the latter analysed imperialism and identified it as the main feature of twentieth-century capitalism. Lenin analysed a phenomenon that Marx did not know, and neglecting him is totally unwarranted, especially for someone wishing to treat the problem of imperialism and 'underdevelopment'. It might also be said: In omitting Lenin from your discussion, you separate Marxism from Leninism, and this is the main danger in your method. Separating the two is a distortion and perversion of both, and untenable in sound Marxist thought.

With regards to this [apparent] defect, our possible and simple response is: We are in no way trying to separate Lenin from Marx. We affirm that Lenin, especially in his great book, *Imperialism: The Highest Stage of Capitalism*, develops Marx's line of thinking that treated capitalism and addressed colonialism, i.e. where he treats imperialism from the perspective of capitalism as a necessary historical development [of capitalism]. If we mention Lenin only briefly, this is based on the fact that we, on this particular point, do not distinguish between him and Marx. Conversely, we find in [Lenin] the natural extension of the author of *Capital*. Our purpose in this research is not to study the founders of Marxism themselves, but to borrow from them to understand our historical reality. It was thus natural for us not to cite a text unless it clarifies 'underdeveloped' reality, the subject of our research. Our goal is reality in light of the text, not the text itself.

necessity to become an actuality; he does not even pose the question, which is perfectly consistent with the logic of the emergence and formation of his thinking. Had Marx examined these latter causes, he would have necessarily had to analyse the socio-economic structure of the countries colonised, especially in their historical relation with the capitalist structure. Marx does not go down this path of inquiry because his primary objective was confined to analysing capitalism, and because – most importantly – the theoretical evolution of this analysis had supposed absolutely no knowledge of the laws governing the evolution of the socio-economic structure of colonised countries. The evolution of theory is [driven] by its own necessity, governed by an inner logic independent of individual will. This does not mean that [theory evolves] in isolation from reality or total independent from it. On the contrary, it means that it does in relative independence defined by what may be called an intellectual field, by which I mean the field of intellectual activity that constituted the historical reality of its structure and becoming. In the movement of its formation and the form in which Marx produced it, the theory of capitalism did not have any realistic potential of taking into consideration the particular structure of colonised countries, because doing so was not necessary to this theory's formation. The cause of this theoretical impossibility is not theoretical, but historical. This is because capitalism, in the movement of its colonial expansion and consolidation for the first time in world history, was history's driving force and the one acting on it. The rest of the world was nothing more than a field on which history acted, not where history was made. In the movement of its becoming, capitalism was not influenced by (even as it influenced) the structure of the countries that it expanded to and transformed. Stated more precisely, while capitalism effected a radical transformation in the structure of the countries it subdued, the transformation that occurred in capitalism's structure as a result of the movement of its own historical expansion was not a transformation as such. It was merely the historical actualisation of the realistic possibilities [inherent in] capitalism's becoming. The transition of capitalism in the movement of its evolution to the imperialist stage cannot be considered a transformation in the structure of capitalism – in the true sense of the word transformation – because it is the realisation of the possibilities that define capitalism in its essence. Capitalism is not capitalism if we take away this possibility. As for the effect of capitalism on the transformation of the structure of colonised countries, we cannot consider it in any way, shape, or form to be the realisation of possibilities [inherent] in their development and becoming. In fact, this transformation is, before anything else, a halting of the movement of these countries' development according to the logic of their inner becoming. It is thus a change in the historical trajectory of their development and a detour away from the horizon of their becoming. Indeed, [this transformation] is a new departure for the history of these countries on new grounds and within a new spatial-temporal structure. In his production of a theory of capitalism, it was not for Marx to pay attention to the structure of this becoming, because this structure did not begin to attain its particularity except after the wars of [anti-colonial national] liberation. Throughout the nineteenth century and up to the outset of the twentieth, the evolution of capitalism continued to be subject to its specific laws, in isolation, so to speak, from the becoming of colonised countries. This is because their particular becoming was nothing more than an extension of capitalism and its specific development.

In the wake of the wars of [national] liberation, through which colonised peoples entered the field of history rather than remain a field of its action, i.e. after they became agents rather than recipients of history, isolating capitalism's trajectory of becoming from that of the liberated countries became impossible. It thus simultaneously became possible to consider the two trajectories of becoming within a contradictory or dialectical unity, bound in a relationship of mutual transformation, within the movement of a single struggle. We can therefore say that the theory of 'underdevelopment' at hand is a practical necessity for driving this conflict forward. It did not become possible except by the entrance of colonised peoples into history. [*The theory of underdevelopment*] *is thus another face of the theory of capitalism, or, we might say, it is the determination of capitalism as it exists through its historical effects*.

Alongside the general definition of the essence of colonialism – as a historical necessity for the evolution of capitalism – we find in [Marx's] *Capital* numerous observations in which Marx treats this colonial relation from different angles, but always through the movement of capitalist production. We do not mean to address all that Marx wrote on this topic, but to distil some of his important observations that stand to help us define the colonial relation as a relation of production from our particular perspective. Defining this relation is nothing other than an attempt to define the particular becoming of colonised countries.

The colonial relation appears first and foremost in the colonies' dependency, a total economic dependency on the capitalist colonising nations. This is the known aspect of the particular relation of production. In his discussion of capitalism's foreign trade and its necessity, Marx states the following: 'By ruining handicraft production of finished articles in other countries, machinery forcibly converts them into fields for the production of its raw material. Thus India was compelled to produce cotton, wool ... for Great Britain'. 'A new and international division of labour springs up, one suited to the requirements of the main industrial countries, and it converts one part of the globe into a chiefly agricultural field of production for supplying the other part, which remains a pre-eminently industrial field'.[4]

This aspect of the colonial relation is well-known, and there is no need to highlight it more. However, we want to draw attention to an important point, especially as it relates to the subsequent progression of our study. A global division of labour assumes the existence of the world as an organic unity whose parts, despite their difference and divergence, interlink and overlap. On the one hand, the trajectory of every part of this unity is determined by the trajectory of the whole, which is simultaneously determined by the trajectory of each of its constituent parts. On the other, we must observe that this unity, even if it appears as the base from which the colonial relation evolves, is actually a historical outcome of this relation as a relation of production, i.e. a historical product of the movement of capitalism's development. Western capitalism is what united the world and its history by uniting the foreign market as a market for its manufactured goods. By tying the becoming of colonised countries to the movement of Western capitalism's own historical evolution, Western capitalism simultaneously linked its own becoming to the movement of these [colonised] countries' historical evolution. Western capitalism thus bound its history to that of its colonies when it bound their history to itself. This inner structural link between the two trajectories of becoming turned the history of humanity into a movement of a coherent totality that is hard to divide or isolate [into separate constituents]. If such separation were to happen, it would be due to the methodological necessity [posed by the task of] defining the becoming of a particular country within the becoming of the larger totality. The existence of the totality is a principal condition for this separation, which is not possible except within the totality. It therefore became impossible to define the structure of the colonised countries' specific trajectories of becoming except within the colonial relation. What was possible before this relation became impossible after. This is what is novel in the structure of these countries' history.

Marx's text thus brings two characteristics of the colonial relation to light: [Firstly], that the colonial relation is a relation of economic dependency, and [secondly], that the historical unity of the world is both the starting point and outcome of this relation.

---

4 Marx 1967, *Le Capital*, Vol. 1, Part 4, pp. 131–2. Paris: Éditions Sociales. (Throughout this study, we draw from this French edition of *Capital*). [Editor's note: For English version of quoted text, see Marx 1982, pp. 579–80 in the Penguin Edition].

There is another aspect of this relation that Marx touches on while discussing foreign trade. He did not intend to analyse this aspect in and of itself, but it is utterly vital for the economic future of colonised countries. It is of such great significance because it still characterises the form of the relation of production between 'underdeveloped' and capitalist countries. Marx states:

> ... And whereas the expansion of foreign trade was the basis of capitalist production in its infancy, it becomes the specific product of the capitalist mode of production as this progresses, through the inner necessity of this mode of production and its need for an ever extended market ...
>
> Capital invested in foreign trade can yield a higher rate of profit, firstly, because it competes with commodities produced by other countries with less developed production facilities, so that the more advanced country sells its good above their value, even though still more cheaply than its competitors. In so far as the labour of the more advanced country is valorized here as labour of a higher specific weight, the profit rate raises, since labour that is not paid as qualitatively higher is nevertheless sold as such. The same relationship may hold towards the country to which goods are exported and from which goods are imported: i.e. such a country gives more objectified labour in kind than it receives, even though it still receives the goods in question more cheaply than it could produce them itself ...
>
> The privileged country receives more labour in exchange for less, even though this difference, the excess, is pocketed by a particular class, just as in the exchange between labour and capital in general. Thus in as much [sic] as the profit rate is higher because it is generally higher in the colonial country, favourable natural conditions there may enable it to go hand in hand with lower commodity prices ...
>
> But this same foreign trade develops the capitalist mode of production at home, and hence promotes a decline in variable capital as against constant, though it also produces overproduction in relation to the foreign country, so that it again has the opposite effect in the further course of development.[5]

We did not quote this entire text because it is lengthy and only indirectly related to our subject. Instead, we selected a few sentences that we will take as a basis for explicating a few important aspects of the colonial relation. This text's full

5 Marx 1967, *Le Capital*, Vol. 3, Part 1, pp. 250–1 [Marx 1991, pp. 344–6, in the Penguin Edition].

title is 'Foreign Trade', and it is a section of a chapter in which Marx examines the causes that hinder the movement of capitalism's primary law. This is the law of 'the tendency of the rate of profit to fall', knowledge of which is crucial to understand the text before us.

This text affirms what we have stated previously, namely that Marx's principal concern is discerning the laws of capitalism's development, given that this evolution was the primary, perhaps only, form taken by global development. In his incidental treatment of the colonial relation, Marx does not examine how this relation develops within the mode of production in colonised countries, nor does he find it necessary to do so. In light of this, we are fully aware of the risk posed by our attempted analysis of Marx's writings, namely that we read into the text what it does not, or is unable to, signify. Our train of thought is, however, methodologically sound. It is the only one to achieve a Marxist understanding of Marx.

This passage [by Marx] presents us with an idea that we had already extracted through analysis, from the first text by Marx. It is the notion that the evolution of world history in its all-encompassing movement is a dialectical unity. In the first paragraph of this text, Marx states that the foreign trade which was the basis of the capitalist mode of production, i.e. its foundation and condition of possibility, came to be – over the course of this production's development – its effect. This means that capitalist production, after being produced by foreign trade, became, by necessity of its internal development, the producer of foreign trade as an ever-expanding horizon. Each produces the other within the movement of its production of itself, i.e. within the movement of its actualisation of its own development. The movement of this reciprocal production is in fact a reciprocal and recurring movement of production.

How does this [latter text of Marx] relate to the former, and how can we prove that the two ideas are actually one? Where is the resemblance between the two? The answer to the first question is simple if we become fully aware of what the first text had led us to. There, we saw that the colonial relation is determined as a relation of economic dependency that links the colonised country to the capitalist colonising country in a single movement of historical development. In this [latter] text, we find the structural unity of history of these two worlds, capitalist and colonial, expressed in another form. Capitalism unifies the world through the development of foreign trade. The foreign trade of capitalist production is nothing but the colonisation of the world and its introduction into a colonial relation with this [capitalist] production. This relation is the only form that capitalism's foreign trade takes with a country whose production is 'underdeveloped'. This structural link and interpenetration between these two unequal [systems of] production – capitalist and colonial – via foreign trade, clarifies the nature of the colonial relation. If we look at capitalist production in its relationship with colonial production, we see that it is not merely the production of commodities that possess a determined social relation. Before all else, *it is the production of a determined social relation, namely the colonial* relation. If the colonial relation is a basis and foundation of capitalist production, then the movement of this production's evolution, as a movement of recurrence and continuity, turns this relation into a product of this system, which had at first been based on [this very relation]. Put more precisely, it can be said that the *structural and historical* unity of colonial and capitalist production renders the former's development as colonial production both a basic condition and product of the latter, and vice versa. There is no course for the development of either except within its relation with the other, *and severing this relation between them is the first necessary condition for transcending, i.e. destroying, both.*

Some might say that we are distorting Marx's text with our interpretation and inference of ideas that it does not contain. So let us look at the text closely to test the soundness of this objection. From the text's first paragraph, Marx is speaking about foreign trade and its relationship with the capitalist system of production. He sees in this trade the production's foundation at its very beginning, i.e. at the outset of its historical formation. In this instance, he is addressing the movement of capitalism's historical formation, not the movement of [capitalism's] internal development following its historical completion. This much is proven by his use of the phrase 'in the beginning'. How, then, can colonial production, from a historical perspective, be the foundation of capitalist production even though it is in reality, i.e. historically, the result of capitalism and its highest phase of development? There appears to be an ambiguity, in this text, or a distorted interpretation. This is not the case. The issue differs according to the perspective we take towards this text.

In other words, it differs according to how we position ourselves in surveying the problem of foreign trade's relation to capitalist production. This is because the issue appears differently based on which aspect one sees it from: the historical versus what we might call the structural front. Each has its own logic. From the historical perspective, i.e. that of capitalism's historical development, capitalism appears, without a doubt, as an outcome of foreign trade's development, which had not yet taken its colonial form in the precise meaning of the word for the simple reason that capitalist production had not yet completed its historical formation to the point at which it can emerge from its own particular foundations. In this phase of capitalism's historical development, we cannot really talk about the colonial relation. This is because foreign trade, as the product of the development of capitalist production, only appeared after the latter's structural features were determined once and for all, at which point its development emerged from its own fixed foundations in accordance with its internal laws. Here necessarily comes the transition to the other, structural front. The logic of historical formation is different than that of structural formation, just as the logic of the history of capitalism's formation is different than that of the history of its development following its formation. Each of these two histories is governed by particular laws that differ from the laws governing the other history. This is why we have examined the text from the perspective of the structural rather than the historical aspect, since what interests us in our attempt to understand the colonial relation is not its history, despite the importance of such knowledge of this history, but, rather, its structure. The most important manifestation of this structure is the unity of the contradictory trajectories of becoming between capitalist production and colonial production. To understand 'underdevelopment' and its becoming, we must begin from this unity, i.e. the colonial relation as a relation of production.

The last paragraph of the quoted text clearly supports our interpretation. There, Marx states that foreign trade, in its colonial form, contributes to the development of the capitalist mode of production. In other words, foreign trade supports the foundations of this production, and sustains it. This means that colonial production, in its relation with capitalist production via foreign trade, is not content with the production of raw materials that are exported for capitalist manufacturing. *Rather, before all else, it is the making of a relation of production that perpetuates this production as colonial production.* Thereby, the relation between capitalist and colonial production is necessarily a circular relation that locks itself in a constantly recurring movement of development. So long as this relation exists between the two [systems of] production, neither may open up unto new horizons. Put otherwise, there is no way for it to transcend to a new mode of production. Capitalist and colonial production open only towards one another. This movement of opening is in fact a closing, or, to use more exact terms, it is a stoppage of development within the colonial relation, since the movement of development of either kind of production always clashes with this relation, which constitutes its internal boundary. The existence of this boundary inevitably guarantees that the foundations of this development remain fixed and immutable. Or, we can say that these foundations do not take on different manifestations except within this boundary, the existence of which preserves them. With regard to colonial production, is this not the basis of what is called 'the vicious cycle' of 'underdevelopment'? Anticipating the conclusion of our study, we will summarise what is relevant therein: *Transcending colonial and capitalist production necessarily occurs with the sever-*

ing of the colonial relation. In other words, the transition to socialism, whether in 'underdeveloped' or capitalist countries, happens inevitably with the severing of this relation, that is by revolting against it. The revolution against colonialism is the only path to liberate human history.

Let us return to the text that we have not left for a moment. We have said that the colonial relation is a relation of production. But what is the economic content of this relation? This relation, as Marx defines it, is one of exploitation by a capitalist country of a colonised country. Put more precisely, it is a relation of overexploitation. This is because the relation exists between two unequally developed countries. From here, we can say that every relation connecting a developed, capitalist country to an undeveloped or generally 'underdeveloped' country via foreign trade or investment by 'capitalists' must necessarily take a colonial form that favours the capitalist country. This is because the [capitalist] country obtains from its colonised or 'underdeveloped' counterpart a greater amount of labour in the form of commodities than the amount of labour it exports to the colonised country in the form of products. The exchange of commodities between the two countries is in reality an unequal exchange that always favours the capitalist country, i.e. that is always in the interest of the more [highly] developed country. This is because the said exchange is of two unequal amounts of labour. The difference between these two [amounts] determines the extent of overexploitation of the 'underdeveloped' country. Even if this difference, (of overexploitation) returns to a specific class in the capitalist country (the bourgeoisie) it still favours the capitalist country as a whole because it contributes to its capitalist development and consolidation. We are not distorting the truth when we say that the development of Western Europe, and the development of the capitalist West generally within the colonial relation, was a historical outcome of the 'underdevelopment' of colonised countries (of Asia, Africa, and Latin America) just as the 'underdevelopment' of these countries is the historical result of Western capitalist development.

Marx's text contains another observation that we must pause to reflect on. He states that the colonised country, in its colonial trade relationship with a capitalist country, receives commodities that is worth, in terms of labour value, less than those received by the capitalist country in exchange. Despite that, i.e. despite this overexploitation, the colonised country obtains commodities [from the colonising country] under better conditions than those under which it would have had to produce or is capable of producing on its own. In other words, the commodities are worth less as imports than as products. It would thus seem that the colonial relation, as a productive relation, is not only in the interest of the colonising country, but also its colonised counterpart. Is this truly the case? The answer to this question really lies in the analysis of the structure of 'underdevelopment' as a particular system of production. We cannot perform this analysis at the present stage of our study, however, before we finish defining the colonial relation in its structure. Our extensive examination of a particular aspect of this definition has ultimately led us to define one of many aspects of 'underdevelopment'. This progression, of our study, interruptions included, is not intentional or personal as much as it is a reflection, in theoretical discourse, of the reality of the structural link between the colonial relation and 'underdevelopment'. We consider it proof of the existence of this link. Research, however, has its methodological exigencies, so we will preserve some cohesion. We feel compelled to answer this question in haste to explain some points without treating the subject in its entirety.

What Marx says about commodities is correct, but this does not at all mean that the colonial relation is in the interest of the colonised country or the development of its production. On the contrary, this relation blocks every prospect of production for the colonised country by keeping it in a continual, structural state of lack in which it cannot compete in any capacity with products [of the capitalist country]. Moreover, the colonial relation prevents the colonised country from engaging in battles of production and competition because the outcome of the battle is always already known. So long as the colonial relation exists, it ultimately favours [more highly] developed production. This relation is, so to speak, a historical deterrent force that paralyses every movement to develop colonial production. It can thus be said that the development of production in a colonised or 'underdeveloped' country ensues only upon severing the colonial relation.

Let us pose our question yet again, but in a different form: As far as the 'underdeveloped' countries are concerned, who benefits from the existence and continuation of the colonial relation? [In other words,] the relation's survival and continuation is in the interest of which class in an 'underdeveloped country'? [The answer is] it favours whomever has a direct tie to capitalist production, i.e. whomever the movement of colonial commercial exchange, meaning the movement of the 'underdeveloped' country's overexploitation by capitalist production, passes through. Before all else, the survival and continuation of the colonial relation are in the interest of the 'underdeveloped' bourgeoisie, which is necessarily determined as a mercantile bourgeoisie. This bourgeoisie is determined as a class exclusively through its connection to capitalist production within the colonial relation. This means that its existence as a class is not an independent sort of existence in the scientific sense of a class. Rather, it is the *representation* of another class existence, i.e. that of the capitalist bourgeoisie. The 'underdeveloped' bourgeoisie represents the capitalist bourgeoisie, lacking in its own class existence the foundations that would constitute it as a class. We therefore wonder to what extent defining it as a class is legitimate in every sense of the word [class]. [Exploring] the 'underdeveloped' bourgeoisie's particular class existence will help us clarify several problems related to the structure and becoming of 'underdevelopment'. For now, it is sufficient to gesture to this point and its major significance without expanding further, as we will do that over the course of our study of 'underdevelopment'.

Through our analysis of some of Marx's writings, several manifestations of the colonial relation's existence as a relation of production have come to light. Throughout our study of these various manifestations, we have tried to reach a basis point, which is that the relation of production is ever inclined towards merging the two structurally different [systems of] production into a contradictory historical unit that renders each system dependent on and inseparable from the other in the course of each system's becoming. If this statement about the structural cohesion of the two systems of production and the unity of their development is right, then the economic dependency that we identified as characteristic of colonial production is also a characteristic of capitalist production. Dependency is thus mutual, even though its form and effects differ between one production and the other. There are thus two points here we must emphasise: the first is the existence of the two systems of production, colonial and capitalist, within a single structural unit. This is what we mean by mutual dependency. The second point is that the development of this structural unit is unequal. The principle of unequal development is one of the most important, fundamental principles of Marxism-Leninism. We find it at the heart of the colonial relation, determining the form of its historical development. If dependency for the colonising country took the form of control and domination, then for the colonised country it is a form of slavery under which the country does not possess mastery over its history. It does not hold the reigns. Moreover, this dependency galvanises the productive forces of development in the colonising country while restricting their development in the colonized country. Rather, it is more accurate to say that it paralyses and cripples them. The more it had a positive effect for the former [metropolitan country], the more negative its effect was on the latter, and vice versa.

In another passage by Marx, we read the following: 'By constantly turning workers into "supernumeraries", large-scale industry, in all countries where it has taken root, spurs on rapid increases in emigration and the colonization of foreign lands ...'.[6]

6 Marx 1982, p. 579. Amel cites it as follows: Karl Marx, *Capital*, Vol. 1, Part 2, p. 131.

This passage is taken from the core of the first text we cited. What concerns us here is not the problem of the global division of labour under the aegis of the colonial relation, but something else that is inextricably linked to issues pertaining to the revolution of [anti-colonial] liberation and its relation to proletarian revolution. Marx states that colonisation is necessary for the development of large-scale industry in the capitalist country. We do not mean to repeat ourselves in reiterating this idea, but to clarify an aspect of it that we have not yet discussed. Development of large-scale capitalist industry does not need colonialism only for purposes of turning manufactured goods into capital and creating an ever-expanding market for them, but also to solve the problem of unemployment, produced by this development, in the capitalist country. If the first aspect of colonialism is known, this latter aspect has barely been treated. It is as if there is something shameful in doing so for revolutionary thought that compels it to avoid rather than tackle the issue. The problem here is truly obscure.

European industry cast a sector of the proletariat out of the production process. That sector's existence was no longer necessary to production, not even in the form of a reserve army. Indeed, it became an obstacle to production after having been an instrument of production. We should not forget that what Marx calls a reserve army is relatively limited, and determined by the cyclical movement of capitalist production. This reserve army of unemployed workers is necessary if production recommences, after its cyclical crisis, in the movement of expanding and flourishing. If the number of unemployed workers, however, exceeds what is necessary for production, there is no solution left to the surplus other than their immigration or dissolution in one way or another. This is precisely what happened in the nineteenth century. Part of the working class, or more accurately of the sector that comprised the reserve army, emigrated to colonise other countries located within what we today call the 'Third World'. This historical phenomenon poses several problems that are beyond the scope of our study. It is enough for our purposes to allude to it, pointing to what could be relevant to our topic. How might we approach, in class terms, this sector of the proletariat that settled the colonies? Must it be considered a part of the European proletariat, or a part of the colonised country's 'proletariat'? In the second case, to what extent did it fuse with the toiling classes of the colonised country? What class position did it take towards the problem of anti-colonial struggle? To speak more broadly, the problem posed here is one of defining the class-based and cultural belonging of this sector of the European proletariat *in light of the colonial relation*. This historical phenomenon bears on our study only insofar as it helps us clarify the true meaning that must be assigned to the liberation movement as an anti-colonial revolution aiming to liberate the colonised man (*al-insan al-musta'mar*), i.e. to transform him. The colonial relation between the colonising and colonised worlds is not merely an economic relation, but an all-encompassing relation, of which the economic aspect is dominant. Had it been merely economic, the relation between the settler proletariat and the toiling masses of a colonised people would not have arisen as an issue. The attitudes of the former would have been identical with that of the forces rebelling against colonial domination, and precedence would have been given to the class struggle in its European capitalist form over the class struggle of liberation, which is the class struggle in its colonial form. This does not match historical reality. For example, what happened in Algeria over the course of the revolution, especially in its later stage, forces us to adopt a concept of class struggle specific to this colonised country that completely differs from its conventional form in capitalist Europe. If we were not to do so, how would we explain the political position taken by the masses of *pied-noirs*, the term used to refer to European settlers in Algeria, against the Algerian revolution? Whether a labourer, artisan, employee, bourgeois, or farmer, nearly every European settler in Algeria was opposed to the revolution of liberation. The animosity [towards the revolution] took a violent form, which reached its peak in the fascist, terrorist 'Organisation de l'armée secrète' (OAS) before independence was won. Oddly, 'Bab El Oued', Algiers' working-class European neighbourhood, had previously been nicknamed 'the red neighbourhood' because it was arguably the main popular base of the communist party before the revolution. Then, after the breakout of the revolution of liberation (i.e. after the central national contradiction erupted), this same neighbourhood became a haven of European racism as well as the home-base and centre of fascist European terrorism against the revolution.

The fact that the principal contradiction in the social colonial structure lies in the realm of national anti-colonial struggle does not at all negate that this movement of contradiction is one of class struggle. On the contrary, [the national contradiction] is the historical form taken by the class struggle in a colonial society. Moreover, this absolutely does not mean that class contradiction was substituted by a 'nationalist contradiction'. This is a reactionary, bourgeois idea that seeks to negate the class struggle in a colonial society and in the struggle's movement towards national liberation. What we mean to emphasise here is that the existence of class struggle, in any social structure, is a particular existence. The struggle for national liberation is the *sole* historical form that distinguishes class struggle in the colonial [structural] formation. Whoever misses this essential point in the movement of our modern history and attempts to substitute class struggle with 'nationalist struggle' or reduce the national struggle to a purely economic struggle loses the ability to understand our historical reality and thus also [the ability] to control its transformation. This is precisely what happened with those who thought that the possibility for the liberation of colonised man and his world from the colonial relation would open up through economic struggle alone. As a result [of this kind of thinking], this form of struggle tended indirectly to preserve the colonial relation. This is because, in practice, this struggle presupposed the existence of the colonial relation. More than that, the relation itself delimited the potentiality of the struggle as economic even when liberation is brought about only by political, (and not economic) struggle, whose goal is to sever this relation. The mistaken assessment of the colonial relation as limited to its economic manifestation is based on a mistaken definition of the economic struggle as direct political struggle. The difference between these two kinds of struggles, however, is massive. The defining feature of political struggle as a class struggle is its fundamental aim of rupturing the social structure's development and initiating its transition to a higher-stage structure. The economic struggle, on the other hand, assumes this structure's existence and continuation. Transition occurs only through revolutionary violence by way of a class struggle that, as we see it, necessarily takes the shape of a liberation struggle.

Those who want to ignore class reality are also mistaken in their definition of the national movement as a merely 'nationalist' movement in which all class struggle disappears. The substitution of class struggle, in its particular liberatory form, with 'nationalist' struggle has a class connotation. It defines a specific class position of a specific class, namely the petite bourgeoisie, towards the problem of colonial liberation. As we will see in our study of 'underdevelopment', this class, by virtue of its structure, aims to paralyse every movement of class differentiation through an attempt to render its own class structure as the social structure [of society as a whole]. Its class ideal is not the dissolution of all classes, which is the proletariat's solution, but the preservation of classes without struggle, i.e. in peaceful coexistence. The only way of achieving this peaceful inter-class coexistence is to stop the movement of development within them, i.e. to stop the dialectical social movement, and to define the petite bourgeoisie as the class standard for all classes, i.e. as the upper limit for their becoming. It is as if the petite bourgeoisie aims to make all classes into a single class that shares its constitution. This equalisation of classes happens on the level of the petite bourgeoisie, thus turning all class identification into identification with this class alone. Therefore, the designation of the national liberation movement as a 'nationalist' movement in which the 'nationalist' character overshadows the class character, or in which the class struggle almost ceases to exist, is in itself a class-based designation and a product of petit bourgeois ideology.

We have not yet examined the most fundamental aspect of the colonial relation. In defining it, we will rely upon an important text by Marx. There, our author states the following:

> ... the same circumstance that produces the basic condition for capitalist production, the existence of a class of wage labourers, encourages the transition of all commodity production to capitalist commodity production. To the extent that the latter develops, it has a destroying and dissolving effect on all earlier forms of production, which, being pre-eminently aimed at satisfying the direct needs of the producers, only transform their excess products into commodities. It makes the sale of the product the main interest, at first without apparently attacking the mode of production itself; this was for example the first effect of capitalist world trade on such peoples as the Chinese, Indians, Arabs, etc. Once it has taken root, however, it destroys all forms of commodity production that are based either on the producers' own labour, or simply on the sale of the excess product as a commodity. It firstly makes commodity production universal, and then gradually transforms all commodity production into capitalist production.[7]

Elsewhere in the same book, Marx writes:

> ... the capitalist mode of production is conditioned by modes of production lying outside its own stage of development. Its tendency, however, is to transform all possible production into commodity production; the main means by which it does this is precisely by drawing this production into its circulation process; and developed commodity production is itself capitalist commodity production. The intervention of industrial capital everywhere promotes this transformation, and with it too the transformation of all immediate producers into wage-labourers.[8]

In this passage, Marx reveals to us the essence of the colonial relation insofar as it is a structural relation between two different [systems of] production: capitalist and non-capitalist or pre-capitalist. By the latter kind of production, we mean what prevailed in colonised countries before they were colonised. Marx is content in this text to define this production as pre-capitalist production.

7 Marx 1992, pp. 119–20. Amel cites it as follows: Karl Marx, *Capital*, Vol. 2, Part 1, pp. 37–8.
8 Marx 1992, p. 190. Amel cites it as follows: Karl Marx, *Capital*, Vol. 2, Part 1, p. 102.

This does not mean that he did not address the prevalent systems of production in these countries before their colonisation. Indeed, there are many places in *Capital* where he attempts to sketch for us the features of the private mode of production that prevailed in these countries, namely the 'Asiatic Mode of Production'. If he did not consider [in detail] this system of production in the course of his reference to the colonial relation, it is because he viewed this relation, as we stated before, as a necessity for the development of capitalist production. In his definition of the colonial relation and its effect on the socio-economic structure of colonised countries, therefore, he did not think about production in these countries except as pre-capitalist production lagging behind capitalist production. He thus specified [this pre-capitalist production] in a negative rather than a positive way. This negative definition made capitalist production both the standard for all previous production and the model for its development. This reflects Marx's view that all production which existed before capitalist production necessarily becomes productive and capitalist if it enters into a relationship with capitalist production, a relationship that necessarily took a colonial form.

The basic idea in this text may be summed up as follows: The development of the colonial relation is at its basis a movement of structural transformation of the system of production which becomes tied to capitalist production via foreign trade. This transformation is in reality the 'capitalisation', so to speak, of production in the colonised country. The movement of this 'capitalisation' [is complicated]. It does not happen at once but through two stages: The first is the generalisation of commodity production in colonised countries. This generalisation is the direct effect of global trade as capitalist trade. In the second stage, the transformation of commodity production into capitalist production occurs. It is worth noting here that the movement of the 'capitalisation' of colonised countries' production is realised within a movement of demolition and dismantling of these countries' socio-economic structure. This means that the development of capitalism in our countries was not the result of a 'natural' development in the system of production that predated their colonisation as much as it was an effect of their colonisation. In other words, it was an effect of the historical and structural linkage of these countries – by way of the colonial relation – to capitalist production. There is ample historical evidence of this. Private property, for example, was unknown in countries like Egypt or Algeria before they were colonised. Colonisation cut the thread of continuity in our history and sent through it violent tremors, the shock of which we are still suffering and living through. Colonisation is what introduced into our countries the contradiction without which there is no history. Its evolution is our history, the form it took, while the reigning in of this evolution is the imperative [call] for our liberation through liberating our world from colonisation. This is the general idea that we can extract from this crucial text by Marx. But we shall pause to reflect on it a little longer, as we have several remarks to make:

First of all, if 'capitalisation' of production in a colonised country is the direct historical result of the colonial relation, then its movement can only continue within this relation. This means that the development of capitalism in colonised countries is hostage to the continuation of the colonial relation. The existence of the colonial relation appears as a historical and structural necessity for achieving and furthering development. The continuation of this relation is thus a basic condition of the possibility [for development]. This is an extremely important point – practically and theoretically – because it helps us understand in very clear theoretical terms that severing the colonial relation precludes all capitalist development in a colonised or underdeveloped country. It used to be thought that severing this relation would allow the colonised country to achieve national capitalist development, both democratic and independent. Such [national development], it was thought, would repeat the logic of Western capitalist development, when in fact such a severance would be the necessary condition for the country's socialist – I do not say non-capitalist – development. If the colonised country remained underdeveloped after its 'independence', then it is due to the failure to cut off its relation with what kept it in a state of underdevelopment: colonisation.

My second remark elaborates and clarifies the former. Just as capitalism emerged and developed in the colonised country within the colonial relation, the colonial bourgeoisie – ignorantly and erroneously labelled the 'national' bourgeoisie – was likewise constituted as a class under the aegis of this relation. Its class existence is thus structurally and historically connected to the existence of the colonial relation, which in turn is determined as the natural field for the colonial bourgeoisie's class becoming. The colonial bourgeoisie's formation and historical development is absolutely inseparable from the movement of what produced it, namely the 'capitalisation' of production in the colonised country.

This point illuminates the nature (i.e. class structure) of the colonial bourgeoisie, which we can thus define as fundamentally a **mercantile** bourgeoisie. Whether upon its emergence or during its historical development and class becoming, it is impossible for this class to be anything but a mercantile class. The reason for this [impossibility] is rather clear. The colonial relation is the historical framework of the development of the capitalisation of colonial production. The colonial relation is what both limits and determines the historical possibilities for the development of the colonial bourgeoisie. It would therefore be impossible for the mercantile bourgeoisie to become an industrial bourgeoisie over the course of its class development, which is what happened in the West, for example. This [colonial] class was born impotent and paralysed because it was born as a colonial [class]. It was thus destined to remain in a state of undeveloped infancy. We may say that the presence, or more accurately the keeping, of this class in a state of underdevelopment is the only historical form its development may take.

We stated that the main reason it is impossible for the mercantile bourgeoisie to develop into an industrial bourgeoisie in the colonised, underdeveloped country is that this development unfolds within the colonial relation. This is what fundamentally distinguishes the colonial bourgeoisie from the capitalist bourgeoisie, and it gives us cause to question the extent to which it is right to apply the concept of class to this colonised 'class'. It is utterly impossible for mercantile capital to engender industrial capital in a colonised 'underdeveloped' country due to the fact that trade in such a country is inherently colonial, which means that it is trade of exports and imports: the export of raw materials and import of manufactured goods. In the West, the transition of mercantile capital to manufactured capital was enabled by the fact that the movement of this transition was actualised independently, i.e. in isolation of any colonial relation that limited or determined it. The difference between the respective historical becoming of a Western capitalist country and a colonised country is not merely in the development or level of production. The difference lies, rather, in the *structure* of production, and is thus a difference in the *structure* of historical becoming itself. We therefore observe the following: colonial capital, in its transition from its particular form as mercantile capital to finance capital, naturally develops into finance capital representative of imperialist capital. The absence of the industrial link in the movement of colonial capital's development is what fundamentally distinguishes the structure of this capital's becoming. This absence, moreover, is what fundamentally determines the structure of 'underdevelopment'.

We have called the bourgeoisie of a colonised 'underdeveloped' country the 'colonial bourgeoisie'. It is now time to clarify our designation of this specific class. Who comprises this class? Which social factions does it encompass? Attending to the historical form taken by the movement of the capitalisation of production in a colonised country within the colonial relation will help us answer this question. As we have already observed, the principal character of this movement of capitalisation subsisted in the formation and development of mercantile colonial capital. In light of this, it becomes evident why there would be deep class solidarity between the factions of merchants and landowners, who in turn are, or become, merchants because of how production develops and capitalisation takes place within the colonial relation. In other words, the colonial bourgeoisie is a single class made up of two different social factions: merchants, by which we mean urban merchants, and landowners who direct their agricultural production towards colonial trade before anything else. Theoretically and historically, therefore, it is difficult if not impossible to consider this faction of landowners a separate class independent of the urban merchants and call them feudalists. This is [impossible], we argue, because the colonial relation radically changes the structure of pre-capitalist production whereby it eliminates its primitive, traditional forms and forcibly steers it towards capitalist production. Through the development of this relation, it was impossible to consider the agricultural production in an 'underdeveloped' colonised country as feudal production, even if the landowners appeared this way [as feudalists]. Due to its connection to capitalist production via colonial trade, this production became colonial production, i.e. production of the raw materials required by capitalist manufacturing. This is why we cannot consider the landowners, especially the large landowners, feudalists. Any discussion of feudal relations of production in a colonised 'underdevelopment' country that exists within the colonial relation is in grave error born of total ignorance of the effect of imperialist capitalism's development *on the structure of production in the colonised country.*

We have covered this point in our analysis of one of Marx's aforementioned texts, so there is no need to repeat it here. Whoever affirms the existence of feudal relations of production in the colonised country lacks an understanding of the nature of the structure and historical development of the colonial relation. In the colonised country, the connection between colonial and capitalist production might appear as if it were a preservation of the 'feudal' relations of production that predated colonialism there. The famous political saying, 'the feudalism-colonialism alliance', is based on this sorely mistaken, distorted idea. It errs in its identification of feudal relations when there is in fact no feudalism in the colonial relation. It distorts in its separation of the bourgeoisie from the feudalists in a colonised country, which results in the bourgeoisie appearing as an anti-colonial class, or a class potentially opposed to colonialism. This saying is thus purely bourgeois, a product of colonial bourgeois ideology with no relation to Marxist thought. This mistaken understanding would have us believe that colonialism enforces the continuity and preservation of the socio-economic structure in a colonised country, even though, as we saw in a previous chapter by Marx, it actually destroys and dismantles this structure in transforming it towards capitalist production.

This mistaken understanding is nonetheless based in historical reality, and we should attend to it. In its initial phases of expansion, there is no doubt that colonialism found a sturdy bulwark in large landowners, let us call them 'feudalists', as well as in the tribal heads who controlled the communal lands. Colonial [forces] thereby increased landowners' holdings and granted ownership to [tribal leaders]. This occurred in Algeria and Egypt, for example, as well as in parts of Lebanon. Even though this alliance was between landowning farmers and colonialism, it was not between *feudal production* and capitalist production. Rather, it was an alliance of production necessarily slated to become colonial production with capitalist production. Landed property in a colonised country was no longer 'feudal'. Through the development of agricultural production within the colonial relation, landed property developed into colonial property as a specific form of 'capitalist' property. By steering agricultural production in the colonised country towards colonial trade, in other words, through the transformation of agricultural production into colonial production, the preservation of agricultural relations of production within the limits of the colonial relation came to mean the transformation of these relations from 'feudal' relations of production into colonial relations of production. Landowners thus became agricultural merchants linked to colonialist production.

As it relates to the colonised country, the colonial relation's historical development thus reveals itself as a process by which *two different social factions were fused into one class*. These were the 'feudalist' faction – or, more precisely, the landowning faction – and the bourgeois faction. As the result of the colonial relation's development, this process of class unification illuminates the movement of the underdeveloped colonised country's becoming, especially when we compare it to the process of violent class differentiation in the West that pitted the feudalists against the bourgeoisie. We all know that the bourgeois revolution in the West was the result of a violent class struggle between two separate, contradictory classes, namely the feudal and bourgeois classes. The dissociation between these two classes turned the bourgeoisie into an ascending class that took a leading role in the movement and transformation of social production, i.e. its liberation. We should remark that the development of capitalism was historically delayed wherever the contradiction between these two classes was weak, meaning that the movement of differentiation between them was slow and faint, as was the case in Germany over the nineteenth century. The contradiction between these two classes, however, is [not just weak, but] totally lacking in the colonised country for the simple reason that these two different classes do not exist in the colonised country. Instead, they exist as two factions of a single class formed through the development of the colonial relation.

How can we then talk about a bourgeois 'national' revolution or define the potential for proper development of *capitalism* in a colonised, underdeveloped country? Bourgeois revolution is fundamentally impossible in a country enveloped by the colonial relation in its historical development. This is because the class struggle in the colonised country is totally different from the class struggle in a capitalist country. In a colonised, underdeveloped country, the class struggle does not hold any potential for the development of production in a capitalist form, and the development of production does not allow a capitalist form of production to emerge. Its bourgeoisie, moreover, is colonial, not capitalist. Because the colonial bourgeoisie's historical formation took place within the colonial relation as a particular mercantile bourgeoisie that included landowners and urban merchants, it did not become an ascending class like the capitalist bourgeoisie. From the moment of its emergence, the colonial bourgeoisie was determined as a class in decline that must be annihilated for production to be transformed and liberated. It is thus a grave error to define the principal contradiction, or engine, of a colonised, underdeveloped country as that between the feudalists and bourgeoisie. There is, in fact, only one class comprised of these two factions. The difference between them evolves towards a lack thereof. There might be a temporary and interest-based contradiction between factions of a single class, but it is wrong to elevate this possible, secondary contradiction to the status of a principal contradiction, i.e. a contradiction that determines the social structure and its development.

This determination of the colonial bourgeoisie as a particular mercantile bourgeoisie that represents the colonialist bourgeoisie in the 'underdeveloped' country precludes considering it a 'national' bourgeoisie with a leading or so-called progressive role in the movement of anti-colonial struggle. It is perhaps more appropriate to use the term 'national' bourgeoisie in reference to the faction of industrialists 'connected to national production'. The problem, however, still stands with regard to whether it is possible to consider this [industrialist] faction an independent bourgeois class with class characteristics specific to it. It is as if, in designating these industrial elements connected to national production as a specific entity, we mean to emphasise the existence of two different classes, namely the industrial bourgeois class and the financial bourgeois class. If we were to consider these two bourgeoisies as two factions of a single class rather than two independent classes, the problem of the 'national' elements' association with the bourgeois class remains.

The problem of these social elements' class designation presents itself when we define the bourgeoisie in the colonised, 'underdeveloped' country as a colonial bourgeoisie, i.e. as a particular mercantile bourgeoisie. If the movement of this bourgeoisie's historical development does not pass through the cycle of industrial development, then how can we consider this industrial faction that is 'connected to national production' as an inseparable component of the colonial bourgeoisie? In doing so, it is as if we are saying that it is possible for this colonial bourgeoisie, or, rather, a sector of it, to develop production along capitalist lines, even though we denied that it is at all possible for capitalism to develop in a colonised, 'underdeveloped' country. To define this industrial faction as a component of the bourgeoisie would be the conclusion reached by a specific kind of reasoning that attempts to illuminate 'underdeveloped' reality in light of the logic of capitalism's historical development in the West. The mistake in this thought process lies in its application of intellectual paradigms specific to Western capitalist reality to our 'underdeveloped' reality. The presence of a financial bourgeoisie and industrial bourgeoisie in the West is by no means an indication that they exist in an 'underdeveloped' country, for the simple reason that the logic of capitalism's development in the West differs from this logic in an 'underdeveloped' country. In a colonised, 'underdeveloped' country, the industrial faction cannot be defined as either an industrial bourgeois class or as a component of the colonial bourgeois class. This is because, again, capitalist development is impossible for this country so long as it is within the colonial relation. A more scientifically precise definition of this faction would identify it in class terms as a special component of the petite bourgeoisie rather than a component of the bourgeoisie. Our theoretical definition of these elements connected to national production is not just 'philosophical jargon'. Rather, it has serious scientific and political significance. Indeed, it informs our strategic political position towards this specific social class as we steer the class struggle in a revolutionary direction.

We will not prolong our discussion of this point here, as we will return to it in the second section of this study, where we aim to confront the problem of 'underdevelopment'. For now, we will quickly summarise what we mean to say in defining this faction as a special component of the petite bourgeoisie. Attending to the nature of industry in a colonised, 'underdeveloped' country will help us understand what we are confronting here. In countries like ours, industry is closer to craft-like work than it is to the heavy industry we see in capitalism. It is what is called 'light' or *consumerist* industry. As such, it is limited to producing means of consumption and incapable of producing means of production. This is what marks it as 'underdeveloped'. If we were to compare it only to consumerist capitalist production, the difference – both qualitative and quantitative – is plain. 'Underdeveloped' industry is significantly weaker and less centralised, and this is what makes it similar to craftwork. Even its most developed sectors appear weak and frail in comparison to developed consumerist capitalist sectors. We cannot properly evaluate 'underdeveloped' industry in a context shut off from the rest of the world. Rather, we must assess it in light of the global degree of industrial development, especially capitalist industry. If 'underdeveloped' industry were measured against consumerist capitalist industry, the massive disparity between the two would come to light and establish the craft-like quality of the former. This craft-like character of 'underdeveloped' industry is what gives us cause to consider the faction of industrialists in an 'underdeveloped' country, generally speaking, as a special component of the petite bourgeoisie that does not belong to the bourgeois class. There is no way for 'underdeveloped' consumerist industry to develop along capitalist lines that parallel Western industrial development. The existence of the colonial bourgeoisie as a class blocks every path of development for this industry. There must be a class contradiction, therefore, between the petite bourgeois faction of industrialists and the colonial bourgeoisie. This contradiction, however, is not the principal contradiction i.e. driving force in an 'underdeveloped' social formation. Rather, it is a secondary contradiction that develops within the class alliance between the colonial bourgeois and this particular sector of the petite bourgeoisie. We would be gravely mistaken to define this as a principal contradiction, since doing so would be to accept the possibility that this social faction could become an industrial bourgeois class capable of actualising the capitalist development of colonial production. We have already negated this possibility. We can therefore say that the horizon of this social faction's class development is necessarily limited, a limitation determined by the colonial relation.

Having designated the faction of manufacturers as a special component of the petite bourgeoisie, we now ask: what is it that distinguishes this faction in its class existence, i.e. in its belonging to this particular class? The answer is: its desperate attempt to liberate itself from its class chains by transitioning to another class, namely the bourgeoisie. The attempt is doomed to fail thanks to the colonial structure of 'underdeveloped' society. This attempt is inherently a class betrayal, just as the class ideal for this component of the petite bourgeoisie is determined as *a class illusion* based in 'underdeveloped' reality.

In general, i.e. at an abstract level irrespective of any specific historical reality, it is completely natural, for industrial elements to aspire to be an independent industrial class that plays the primary role in actualising social production. The colonial structure of social reality, however, turns this natural aspiration or class ideal into a class illusion. The colonial relation, as we have seen, determines the transformation of these industrial elements. It shuts off the horizon of their becoming as an industrial bourgeoisie. Because industry within the colonial relation will always be consumerist in nature in an 'underdeveloped' country, the horizon of becoming for this component of the petite bourgeoisie is never the industrial, and impossible to exist, bourgeoisie, but the colonial bourgeoisie. Many industrialists in an 'underdeveloped' country are thus simultaneously merchants and financiers. The diverse activities of this social faction are not born of 'excess energy', but of a structural deficiency in the process of concentrating industrial production and expanding it both vertically and horizontally. The ambiguous relationship between this component of the petite bourgeoisie and the colonial bourgeoisie is centred on the particularity of 'underdeveloped' production as consumerist production. This particular type of industry in turn illuminates for us the class position that this productive component of the petite bourgeoisie takes towards colonialism. If, under particular historical conditions, this class were to enter into a contradiction with colonialism, it would be because colonialism was attempting to annihilate this productive component of an [otherwise] unproductive class by exporting [colonialism's] own uncompetitive consumer goods.

In certain circumstances, however, colonialism is able to take a clever position towards this class. It acts as a friend rather than a foe. The development of consumerist industry in an 'underdeveloped' country does not conflict with colonialism in its new form. Instead, it can be the basis for colonialism's development and penetration of the 'underdeveloped' country. This new form of the colonial relation is determined as a new, global division of labour whereby the country which produces primary raw materials can also produce means of consumption while industrial countries produce the means of producing consumer production. This new global division of labour is actually a division of industrial labour within the general global division of labour. This new division determines the old division by keeping it within boundaries which in turn determine the old division. This means that the colonial structure of the 'underdeveloped' country is what determines industry therein as consumerist industry. Its development within the colonial relation in turn determines the colonial character of the 'colonised' country's development, thus keeping it in a state of 'underdevelopment' instead of extracting it from that state. The development of industry in an 'underdeveloped' country as consumerist industry strengthens the structural connection between colonial production and metropolitan capitalist production, making this a basis for that, and that an effect of this, in perpetuity. In light of this structural connection between the two systems of production, it is not strange that we find the productive component of the petite bourgeoisie to be in natural agreement with colonialism. The contradiction between them is incidental, while their alliance is the basis of their class existence. Indeed, the contradiction between them appears only on the basis of their class alliance. This explains the ambiguous, wavering position taken towards colonialism by the productive component of the petite bourgeoisie. It also explains this faction's tendency towards cooperation and collaboration with the representative and embodiment of colonialism in an 'underdeveloped' country: the colonial bourgeoisie.

We began with one of Marx's texts, and his analysis has led us to treat various aspects of the class condition in an 'underdeveloped' country. This is what our particular reading of this text – stated in the introduction – has yielded. Let us now turn to a third observation about Marx's aforementioned text.

In our first remark on this text, we noted that the historical result of the connection between a colonised country's production and capitalist production – via foreign trade and within the colonial relation – was the 'capitalisation' of production in the colonised country. But in our second remark, we noted that the historical development of the colonial relation necessarily closes off every possibility for capitalist development of production in a colonised country. At first glance, it may appear that these are contradictory statements or, more precisely, it would appear that there is a contradiction between what Marx says in the first remark, and what we say in the second remark. The fact of the matter is that these are different, not contradictory, statements. Our statement is nothing more than a particular emphasis on the soundness of Marx's statement. There is no disagreement over the process of 'capitalisation', but over its historical form. This difference is a result of the fact that Marx's studies of capitalism, as we have previously mentioned, do not look at the structure of colonial production in its relation to capitalism. He stops, rather, at defining the structure of capitalist production. There is a difference here because the problem that we are posing is different from that which Marx posed. The difference does not lie in the proposed solution of the problem, but in the problem itself. The problem treated by Marx can be stated in the following form: how is the movement of the influence of capitalist production on colonised countries determined within the development of the colonial relation? The solution to this problem lies in the concept of 'capitalisation' that we have previously discussed. As for the problem that we mean to pose in this study, it can be formulated thusly: What is the historical form taken by the 'capitalisation' of production in a colonised country? In this movement of 'capitalisation', is colonial production historically and structurally identical to the capitalist mode of production?

We have attempted in earnest to clarify and insist upon the fact that the unity between capitalist and colonial production, achieved through the colonial relation, is not a unity of identification, but of differentiation. The movement of this unity's historical development is in reality a movement of structural differentiation between the two [systems of] production, not a movement of identification.

It is very important, theoretically and practically, to emphasise the differentiated nature of the unity of the colonial relation. It is eminently clear that the strategy of our revolutionary work, i.e. the theory of revolution in our society, cannot be established except on scientific knowledge of the structure of colonial production as a particular structure of production. We have thus seen it preferable to consider the movement of production's 'capitalisation' in a colonised country through the development of the colonial relation, as movement of its colonisation rather than movement of capitalisation. In other words, production in a colonised country leans towards turning into colonial production and not towards capitalist production. In fact, this colonial production is nothing but a specific historical form of the particular existence of capitalist production in a colonised, 'underdeveloped' country within the colonial relation. Despite being part of the capitalist system of production, it is thus different from this system both in its structure and in the logic of its development. Our emphasis on the particularity of the colonial structure vis-à-vis the capitalist structure is, therefore, absolutely theoretically necessary to understand our historical reality.

Our brief examination of the colonial relation has led us to an immensely important conclusion, namely that this relation's historical development gave rise to a particular system of production in the colonised country. It is in unison with and belongs to the capitalist system of production insofar as it differs from that system in both its structure and evolution. We defined this system of production as a 'colonial system of production'. It was necessary that this point of arrival be the point of departure for our next study of 'underdevelopment'. The theory of 'underdevelopment' must be defined, therefore, as a theory of a colonial system of production, i.e. as an attempt to define the general laws governing the structure and historical development of colonial production.

CHAPTER 4

Colonialism and Underdevelopment II: On the Colonial Mode of Production

... In his analysis of capitalism's development in Russia, Lenin speaks of the coexistence of several modes of production with the capitalist mode acting as the dominant one.[1,2] This configuration, he says, is the defining characteristic of the social structure in Czarist Russia, especially in its Asian colonies. Lenin's notion of several modes of production coexisting within a single country reveals his deep awareness that colonial reality is complex and irreducible to a single, recognisable mode of production like feudalism or capitalism. A new reality, [Lenin suggests], deserves a new analysis. Lenin highlights an important fact about this reality's structure, namely that feudalism and capitalism did not succeed each other in a chronological manner as they did in the West but, rather, coexisted within a single social formation. According to his analysis, a capitalist system exists within a feudalist framework, and a feudalist framework exists within a capitalist system. This kind of coexistence is a new development in human history. It appeared only in countries subjected to colonial rule at some point during their historical development. Because Lenin's concept of coexistence is more descriptive than analytical, however, it does not solve the problem before us. For how can several different modes of production coexist in a single social structure? And what form does this coexistence take? Can we even say that there is a coherent social structure in such a situation? The concept of coexistence, moreover, presupposes and requires the existence of external relations between modes of production brought together by their

1 Editor's note: In *al-Tariq*'s version of this study, Amel employs the term *nizam al-intaj* (system of production). He later switches to *namat al-intaj* (mode of production). The latter became the title of his expanded study published four years later. We have used both terms interchangeably in the body of the text, often adhering to Amel's formulation, but opted to use his 'mode of production' for the title to signify Amel's eventual choice of words. This study was first published in *al-Tariq* magazine, no. 8, 1968. The translation is based on a reproduction of the study as an appended text to the 2013 edition of Amel's *Theoretical Prolegomena for the Study of the Impact of Socialist Thought on the National Liberation Movement*, first published in 1972.

2 Editor's note: The original Arabic text includes an introductory section that mostly sums up part one of Amel's study *On Colonialism and Underdevelopment*. Given that the first part was translated in full, the introductory section was dropped from this translation of Part 2.

 | DOI:10.1163/9789004444249_005

coexistence within a whole. This, in particular, makes it difficult for us to accept this concept without violating our previous hypothesis. The development of a particular mode of production in the framework of another altered each. Understanding their internal relationship thereby requires understanding the unity rather than multiplicity of the structure they inhabit.

The concept of the coexistence of multiple modes of production reflects the historical reality of the complex colonial structure it describes. When the colonial phase of capitalism reached its zenith in the early twentieth century, the colonial social structure had not yet appeared in its unity as a particular class structure. Generally speaking, a social structure's development as a class structure is always accompanied by the development of class consciousness at the theoretical level. The development of class structure both defines and is defined by this consciousness. The development of this consciousness is at its core a political rather than an intellectual process. It is through practical, i.e. political, struggle rather than detached thought that such a development is achieved. Class consciousness alone is capable of discerning class structure and thereby defining it. If we were to consider the early twentieth-century movement of liberation struggle, we would see that it was still in its infancy, if not absent.

It was only after WWII that national liberation became a great wave that swept across, and was a driving force of, human history, or the history of colonial domination of humanity. Before this period, the struggles of colonised peoples, their intensity notwithstanding, were not yet struggles for liberation. This is because the social contradictions underlying these struggles had not yet merged into a unity whose centrepoint was national liberation. In the struggle for liberation from colonialism, we know that the unification of class struggles (i.e. class contradictions) is an absolutely necessary condition for success. If this unity is lost, the class nature of the struggle itself would be lost, thus precluding each social class involved from taking the struggle to its successful resolution. If the peasants' struggle in colonised countries, for example, were to remain a purely peasant struggle independent from the workers' struggle, and the workers' struggle were to remain separate from the struggle of the rest of the exploited classes, then the liberation movement itself would inevitably fail. This is because the liberation movement is a class struggle against colonialism, which is the principal class enemy of all labouring classes. If class struggle against this single class enemy is not unified into one universal movement, then colonialism remains victorious. The movement for national liberation in the early twentieth-century was generally distinguished by the absence of this unity in the colonised classes' struggle against the colonial powers and their representatives. For this reason, the economic rather than political character of the workers' struggle predominated in many colonised countries, such as Algeria, Egypt, and Cuba.

While political struggle is necessarily a unifying act, economic struggle seldom targets the entirety of the social structure. Under these conditions of a fragmenting and fragmented class struggle, each class of workers in colonised countries (e.g. labourers, peasants, and petit-bourgeois factions) undertook its own struggle independently and in isolation from the others. It is as though each of them belonged to a discrete social structure even though their class enemy was one and the same. This class independence appeared as though it was the outcome of different, independent social structures coexisting within a single colonised country. In reality, however, this was not the case. Rather, this single enemy, namely colonialism, is the *objective basis* for the unity of the colonised country's social structure. The fact that this structural stage [of unity] was not apparent to class consciousness [of the time] does not negate its existence. It is, rather, a sign that the toiling classes' consciousness was underdeveloped. The appearance of the colonial social structure as the coexistence of multiple systems of production merely reflects the way in which this structure was conceptualised at a particular stage of consciousness reached by the toiling classes. During this stage of colonial expansion, the development of expansionist capitalism was the major, unifying motor of history while colonised peoples were its object. At that stage, the class existence of the various classes in colonial societies was essentially fragmented. In other words, these classes' existence was external to the process of historical change, [i.e. a class-in-itself]. The objective and historical conditions for class consciousness to become aware of the colonial social structure had not yet cohered. Classes subjected to colonial domination and exploitation were not yet fully aware that their respective trajectories of class becoming were unified in a shared struggle against colonialism. The process by which structural unity emerges as such in colonial society is one and the same as that of the historical development of the alliance between the exploited classes who share a single trajectory of becoming. This process is thus inextricably linked to the development of class struggle in colonial society. Its conditions are only met by the unification of these classes' struggles into a single liberation struggle. In other words, the unity of the colonial social structure appears to consciousness only when the historical conditions of possibility for its appearance are actualised. These conditions are nothing other than the unity of the liberation struggle.

The unity of the liberation struggle began to materialise in the class struggle of colonial societies when colonised peoples became a motor force of history, particularly after World War II. During this period, the struggles of the exploited classes in colonial societies began to cohere into a universal struggle for liberation. The historical conditions for the unveiling of social reality as a cohesive whole thus also materialised. Before this point, theory could not aptly reveal what reality itself, in the movement of its historical development, had not allowed it to reveal. For this reason, we doubt that the concept of the coexistence of multiple modes of production in colonial society can define this society's structure with precision, especially after the unity of this structure began to appear to class consciousness *practically* in the unity of the struggle for liberation. It is impossible for the struggles of peasants, workers, intellectuals, and a faction of the bourgeoisie to be united in a universal movement if the structure of the society in which this movement unfolds is not a single structure. This is because the unity of the social structure is the basis for the unity of the exploited classes' struggle in colonial society. The unification of these classes' struggle against colonialism, moreover, is out of the question if the mode of production in their society is not a single whole. Indeed, the unity of class struggle is a sign of the unity of the [society's] structure of production. *If this were not the case, then we would not be able to understand the logic of the revolution for liberation and the possibility of its success as a socialist revolution, i.e. as a violent transition from one particular mode of production to another, from colonialism to socialism.*

The concept of the coexistence of multiple modes of production in colonial society expresses a phase in its historical development in which class contradictions in colonial society had not yet erupted into a revolution for liberation. This concept cannot therefore reflect the new phase of history [that concerns us], when the latter began to move in the direction opposite [to colonisation]. It began to unify anew around an all-encompassing opposing movement in which humanity attempted to liberate itself from colonial domination. For this, the concept of a 'colonial mode of production' is most suited for understanding the structure of 'underdevelopment', i.e. for defining the structure of colonial reality as it unfolds in history. This concept is capable of reflecting [the reality of] this new phase defined by the revolution for liberation.

To speak of a colonial mode of production is to assume the existence of a cohesive, distinct social structure. This structure develops according to the logic of its internal contradictions. It does so within a framework out of which history emerges as a revolutionary movement that destroys this very framework [in its march] towards socialist development. This means that the conditions for socialist revolution in colonised countries are born out of the development of contradictions internal to the distinct colonial mode of production in these countries. The socialist revolution in these countries is thus both a revolution against this mode and a result of its historical development. In other words, it is a liberatory revolution against colonial existence. The historical conditions for the crystallisation of this concept as a theoretical tool for understanding the structure of 'underdevelopment' arose alongside the revolutionary tide of the national liberation movement. This is why the concept of a colonial mode of production did not emerge in the colonial phase of this movement. While the revolutionary period of the national liberation movement provides the scientific basis and legitimacy for our hypothesis, its general theoretical basis lies in the works of Marx himself. As we will see in what follows, there is no contradiction in this.

∵

In the first part of his manuscript titled *Grundrisse: Foundations of the Critique of Political Economy*, specifically in the section on 'the general relation of production to distribution, exchange, consumption', Marx states that the fundamental issue raised by this subject is 'the role played by general-historical relations in production, and their relation to the movement of history generally'.[3] Expounding on this, he writes:

> In all cases of conquest, three things are possible. The conquering people subjugates the conquered under its own mode of production (e.g. the English in Ireland in this country, and partly in India); or it leaves the old mode intact and contents itself with a tribute (e.g. Turks and Romans); or a reciprocal interaction takes place whereby something new, a synthesis, arises (the Germanic conquests, in part). In all cases, the mode of production, whether that of the conquering people, that of the conquered, *or that emerging from the fusion of both* [Amel's emphasis], is decisive for the new distribution which arises.[4]

In the chapter from which this excerpt is taken, Marx attempts to show that production plays a fundamental role in determining all other socio-political phenomena, including consumption, distribution, and exchange. Despite the importance of this point, it does not directly bear on our question. What concerns us in this passage is its allusion to 'the role played by general-historical relations in production', and the outcome of the clash between two modes of production linked through a common process of historical development. Marx attempts to clarify this role in relation to the question of conquests he was addressing. The question we are attempting to answer, on the other hand, is

3 Amel relies on the French translation of Marx's work, cited below.

4 Amel's source: Karl Marx 1967, *Fondements de la critique de l'économie politique*. Paris: Anthropos, pp. 26–7 [Marx 1993, pp. 163–4].

as follows: What is the role of colonial conquest in [shaping] the mode of production in colonised countries? We will draw on Marx's text in answering this question.

This text shows us that it is necessary and not merely possible to consider the historical phenomenon of conquest as a clash between two modes of production belonging to conquered and conquering peoples, respectively. The historical reality of conquest does not lie, therefore, in the event of conquest, but in its role in production and its relation to production. From this angle, and in light of the three possibilities mentioned by Marx, let us consider the case of colonial conquest. At first glance, it appears that the colonised country – in its historical development under colonialism – falls under the first possibility, namely that the colonising West was able to impose its mode of capitalist production on colonised countries. As we saw in this study's first chapter, however, historical reality tells us otherwise: that in fact the West blocked the path of capitalist development within these countries by colonising them. This is precisely the point that we mean to highlight. As for the second possibility [described by Marx], it applies to the phase of Ottoman despotism rather than that of capitalist colonialism. The expansionist nature of capitalist development is such that it absolutely precludes this [second] possibility. Our inclination is thus to say that the third possibility outlined by Marx materialised in colonised countries.

As is evident in the above-quoted passage, Marx does not present colonised countries as an example of the third possibility even though colonialism's movement was developing during his lifetime.[5] Perhaps he thought that these countries conformed to the logic of the first possibility. In any case, this does not concern us, as Marx's theoretical logic is clear enough. What interests us in this passage is its reference to the theoretical possibility for the interaction of two modes of production, and the nature of this interaction as a movement of fusion that produces a new mode of production different from those out of which it came. In Marx's text, there are two phrases to which we should pay close attention if we are to truly grasp the depth of Marxist thought. Marx uses the phrase 'synthesis' in reference to the new mode of production. This ambiguous phrase is rooted in its Hegelian source, where it means something very different than it does in Marx's work. In the Hegelian dialectic and idealist scheme, a 'synthesis' retains elements of its original components and does not transform them. The Hegelian concept of 'synthesis' would thus necessarily

5 In the first chapter of this study, we mentioned the theoretical and historical reasons why Marx did not take an interest in the special mode of production in colonised countries, so we will not repeat ourselves here.

lead us to conceive of underdevelopment in colonised countries as a dual structure. We thus prefer to trade this Hegelian term for another word that Marx uses in the above-quoted text to describe the 'something new' that arises from the interaction of two modes of production.

This other term, namely 'fusion', is purely Marxist. Borrowing it from chemistry, Marx uses 'fusion' in several of his foundational writings (e.g. *Capital*) in a sense that stays true to its root meaning. The movement of fusion is a radical transformation of constitutive elements to produce a new cohesive whole that differs from the sum of its parts. Its difference, moreover, does not merely derive from the multiplicity of the elements that constitute it. Rather, it emerges from their transformation. The movement of production is illustrative in this regard. According to the author of *Capital*, production operates through the fusion of its constitutive elements, namely the means of production and labour power. Just as the fusion in production transforms its components, the fusion which occurs in colonised countries between the capitalist mode of production and its 'traditional' counterpart (i.e. the mode of production which prevailed in the colonised country before it was colonised) transforms them to give rise to a new mode of production.

This fusion does not retain the structures of the two constituent modes of production but, rather, transforms both. It follows that in a colonised country, capitalist production does not exist save for the form it develops into under colonialism. Similarly, 'traditional' production – whether feudalist, pseudo-feudalist, or 'Oriental' – does not persist in a colonised country save for the form it develops into – repetitively – under colonialism. This development of two or more [modes of] productions in a framework that is unnatural to each is necessarily a transformation of them all within a unified [social] structure. It is therefore impossible to separate production itself from the framework of its development, since this framework both determines the structure of production and is determined by it in the course of development. It is this structural and developmental cohesion between production and its historical framework that allows us to speak of a particular mode of production in an 'underdeveloped' colonised country. This is what we are calling the 'colonial mode of production'. What distinguishes it from the capitalist mode of production is the framework in which it developed. The colonial mode of production did not develop historically within the framework of capitalism's development in the West – especially not its formative phase – but, rather, within the social structure of the colonial relation.

2 An Analysis of the Class Contradictions in the Colonial Mode of Production (or, an Analysis of the Relations of Production in the Colonial Social Structure)

As we have seen, our hypothesis derives its legitimacy and scientific character from Marxist theoretical foundations. It is based on the possibility stated by Marx that a mode of production can come about through the fusion of two others. In light of this, we have come to see 'underdevelopment' as a truly particular mode of production. It is the result of the colonisation of 'underdeveloped' countries in a historical process which produces a fusion of capitalist and pre-capitalist modes of production within the framework of the colonial relation. At first glance, colonial production appears as a particular mode of production in two respects: firstly, insofar as it is the expansionist development of capitalist production within the pre-capitalist social framework that it penetrated. Secondly, insofar as it is the development of pre-capitalist production within a capitalist social framework in a repetitive manner. For production to continue to develop, it must take place within a framework external to it. For example, the development of capitalist production in a colonial country under the aegis of the colonial relation preserves 'traditional' production through the very process of dismantling and destroying it.[6] The development of 'traditional' production in a repetitive manner is a result of nothing other than the framework of the deformed 'capitalist' (i.e. colonial) production in which this development occurs. This is because this framework blocks and violently distances the horizon for the [non-repetitive] development of 'traditional' production.

With that in mind, we will attempt to analyse the colonial mode of production as a particular mode of production. Analysing a mode of production means analysing its constitutive contradictions. We must therefore inquire into the contradictions of the colonial mode of production and the form of its historical development. Such an analysis requires that we clarify an important point, namely the fact that this mode's contradictions, generally speaking, are exclusive to it because they developed within a foundational structural framework that determines both the development of the colonial mode of production and the particularity of its structure. This structural framework for the development of the mode's contradictions is defined first and foremost by the economic contradiction, which is foundational to the relation between forces

6 In the previously cited article by Yves Lacoste, he mentions that the prominent colonial administrator Hubert Lyautey understood perfectly the survival of French colonialism in Marrakech to be contingent upon the survival of the country's traditional structures, or at least a majority of them.

of production and relations of production within the social structure. This relation, in turn, constitutes the fundamental framework of social development as development of a particular mode of production. This very relation is what gives this development its distinct character. History is a movement that takes place within a determined structural framework, rather than a repetitive, say an ascending or undifferentiated, movement external to such a framework. In light of this, we must begin by defining the colonial mode of production's basic contradiction, which means defining the structural framework for its historical development.

Marx writes in a famous text, 'In the social production which men carry on they enter into definite relations that are indispensable and independent of their will; these relations of production correspond to a definite stage of development of their material powers of production. The sum total of these relations of production constitutes the economic structure of society – the real foundation, on which arises a legal and political superstructure and to which correspond definite forms of social consciousness'.[7]

There are two key ideas in this dense, important text which bear on our topic. The first is the notion of a constant correspondence between the relations of production and productive forces that brings the two together into a contradictory unity of development. The second is the idea that relations of production, in their relation to modes of production, constitute the socio-economic structure, i.e. the foundation for a society's historical development. From this, we gather that a given society's unity and cohesion lies in the unity and cohesion of production within it. What, then, is the form of this unity and cohesion in colonial production? What form is taken by the relation between the forces of production and the relations of production within it?

We did not choose the term 'colonial production' to designate the mode of production in 'underdeveloped' countries for arbitrary or subjective reasons. This choice was not an emotional response to the terms of 'underdevelopment' or 'backwardness' which have been attached to our societies. Were it such [an emotional] response, we would not have equally rejected the new term 'developing countries'. As of late, the latter has become fashionable in economics literature authored by thinkers of the capitalist West keen to avoid hurting our sensitive and troubled feelings! We reject this new term because it is unscientific and does not indicate the distinct mode of production in these countries. When we refer to capitalist, socialist, or feudalist countries, we are

7 Karl Marx 1982, *Contribution à la critique de l'économie politique*. Paris: Éditions Sociales. pp. 5–4 [Marx 1904, p. 11].

making the mode of production in these countries the standard for assessing them structurally and historically. Yet, by referring to a country as developing, on a developmental path, or underdeveloped, one occludes or masks the mode of production within it. Indeed, there is a danger in revealing these countries' mode of production to those attempting to hide it. All of these terms are similarly misleading because they veil the real, structural, and historical reasons for why 'growth' in colonial countries is slow or non-existent. Our choice of the term 'colonial production' was born out of a rational, scientific aim to bring the reasons for 'underdevelopment' to light and to define the dimensions of its development. Our term draws attention to the historical dimensions (i.e. the structural framework) of the full formation of this production.

In colonised countries, the colonial relation constituted the historical framework for the development of the forces of production. Colonialism introduced new relations of production into these countries in a very violent manner.[8] These new relations of production developed and shaped the forces of production. The insertion of new relations of production in colonised countries proceeded through the internal destruction of the pre-existing development structure, i.e. through a radical change in the historical logic of these countries' development. Unlike the capitalist relations of production that emerged through the historical development of feudalism in Europe, the relations of production that emerged in colonised countries were not a necessary outcome of the internal development of the mode of production which preceded colonialism. Because they formed under the aegis of the colonial relation and direct colonial rule, we have labelled them colonial relations of production. It was only by destroying the pre-existing structure of development that colonial-

8 The process of introducing and normalising private property in countries subjected to colonial rule exemplifies this kind of violence. Private property was introduced into these countries by destroying collective property. Colonial powers appropriated land – the most important means of production in the pre-colonial mode of production – for their allies among the notables and tribal leaders. In Algeria, for example, land was given to local elites on the condition that they relinquish political power to the colonisers. Establishing a class of landowners allied to the colonial power was not the final step in this process. The ultimate goal of colonialism was to steal good land from its original owners. This was achieved in one of two ways: either by violent direct means, which entailed driving people from their lands, relegating them to the mountains, and replacing them with European colonists, or by legitimate (i.e. legal) theft achieved through the purchase of land at cheap prices and the subsequent formation of companies tied to banks that would either appropriate the lands directly or rule over their yields through mercantile exchange. The history of the formation of colonial relations of production in colonised countries is a history of colonial violence. This violence took many forms ranging from theft and plunder – legitimate and illegitimate – to murder and genocide, which was the fate met by the natives of Latin America and blacks of Africa.

ism could free the development of productive forces in countries subjected to its rule and then steer them towards horizons of capitalist production. Pre-colonial relations of production, for their part, paralysed rather than enabled the powers of production and pushed history into a repetitive cycle. Colonialism thus appeared as though it were a motive force of history that destroyed the state of stagnation in which colonised countries had existed, freeing the forces of production that had not been able to produce until then. However, this historical phenomenon – one of immense importance to all colonised countries – deserves a reassessment. The fact of the matter is that the transition in these countries from one mode of production to another, specifically from a pre-colonial to colonial mode of production, did not unfold according to the logic of the first mode's trajectory of becoming. Rather, it was the outcome of a change in the inner structure of this trajectory, i.e. the result of twisting the logic of its development as determined by an external power. The importance of this historical phenomenon becomes apparent when we remember that revolution, in the scientific, Marxist sense, is a transition from one mode of production to another, i.e. from one social structure to another.

The transition to the colonial mode of production in colonised countries, however, cannot be considered a revolution in the true sense of the word, since a revolution is history's liberation through the actualisation of its real, inherent potential. Colonialism, on the other hand, was a revolution against these countries' history and a force opposed to them. Rather than moving their history towards liberation, colonialism thwarted the possibilities of development inherent therein. Colonised countries came to history through their colonisation and the development of colonial contradictions in history. Upon arriving to history, however, colonised countries found the horizons of development blocked before them. The very force that brought them to history – violence – was itself what blocked these horizons. Colonialism violated our countries' history and distorted its movement. In 'liberating' this history from stagnation, colonialism drew it towards a horizon of dependency. It therefore constituted a 'revolution' of suppression rather than liberation. The real revolution would necessarily be fought against colonialism with the aim of freeing the forces that colonialism had suppressed. We must therefore seriously question whether it is even possible to conceive of the colonial mode of production as an autonomous, self-sustaining mode of production. The inescapability of this question appears in sharp relief when we take into account two factors: first, the historical conditions in which the colonial mode of production formed; and second, the limited (and ultimately blocked) horizon for development opened up by the productive forces that colonialism freed, albeit in a framework that necessarily deformed the relations of production [cultivated within it]. In insisting upon the urgency of this question, we are not contradicting ourselves. As we will see, the fact that this mode of production can never be considered completely autonomous or structurally independent and must instead be considered in terms of its structural dependency – whether by looking at its historical formation or its internal development – is one of its most distinguishing characteristics.

The 'freeing' of productive forces in colonised countries under the aegis of colonialism's expansionist production was actually a historical deformation of these forces that set the structural limit of their development. This is due to the fact that productive forces were not freed in colonised countries with the creation of capitalist relations of production (as was the case in Europe, for example) but, rather, through the creation of new colonial relations of production. As is clear in the aforementioned text by Marx, forces of production are at their base social relations and cannot be otherwise. These forces do not develop in the abstract, but are determined within a framework of particular relations of production. Social relations of production, specifically, determine the framework for the development of productive forces and shape production generally. As they develop, these social forces cannot transcend the framework constituted by forces of production. Colonial relations of production necessarily and structurally limited the development of the productive forces freed by colonialism. The difference between colonial and capitalist relations of production is vast in terms of both their historical formation and structural makeup. The structural difference between them in fact derives from the difference in the historical formation by which each was constituted. Within the framework of feudalist production, the formation of capitalist relations of production was shaped first and foremost by the development of productive forces. The necessary breakdown of the feudalist framework was thus a condition for both the completion of capitalist relations and freeing of productive forces. The formation of colonial relations of production, on the other hand, was not an outcome of productive forces' necessary development within the framework of pre-colonial production. Due to the impact of colonial violence and destruction, which directed capitalist development in colonised countries towards the path of colonial dependency, the formation of colonial relations of production eliminated the prospects of capitalist development in these countries before productive forces developed there. Colonialism's 'freeing' of productive forces in colonised countries was an act of deforming them. It aborted possibilities of development towards capitalism. This occurred in Lebanon, for example, and continues in many colonised countries today.

We must not forget that colonialism sought first and foremost to prevent the development of all industry in the colonies, even craftwork or light consumerist manufacturing. As a result, the forces of production borne by colonialism in our countries in order to serve its interests and make good on its investment in enslaving our skills could by no means ascend to the level of independence. While productive forces developed in these countries, dependency was the only possible end towards which this development moved. This dependency and utter subjugation of productive forces and their development is what distinguishes colonial production from its capitalist progenitor. In breaking the feudalist framework in which social production had developed, capitalist production effectively freed the forces of social production from the shackles which had bound them during their development within the larger social structure. These forces in turn became independent from the social structure that had formed through them. Such independence is in fact what defines, i.e. is the basis for, the existence of a mode of production as such. The colonial mode of production does not exhibit this defining quality. What distinguishes it as a mode of production is in fact what prevents it from becoming a mode of production, as if its potential of existing as a mode of production is one and the same as the impossibility of it ever being one.

The difficulty we are facing in defining the colonial mode of production is not due to confusion in our thinking, but to an ambiguity at the heart of this distinct production's historical existence. It is a complex historical phenomenon that is difficult to understand theoretically and thus difficult to define scientifically. The reality is that this mode of production, the distinction of which we have insisted upon in naming it the colonial mode production, has very few of the basic constituents of a mode of production as this term is classically understood. For one, its structure and development lack independence. We do not mean to say that it does not submit to a logic of development specific to it that differs from the logic according to which the capitalist mode of production develops. On the contrary, we mean to say that the colonial mode of production's structural and developmental dependency on its capitalist counterpart is the basis for its specificity and difference. The difficulty in analysing the colonial mode of production lies in how we conceptualise this dependency and uncover its structure. All of our inquiry is an attempt to define this form of dependency, and it has yielded the concept of the colonial mode of production. At first glance, it might appear that the dependency at the core of the colonial mode of production invalidates any attempt to understand it as distinct from the capitalist mode of production upon which it depends. If this were true, i.e. if the appearance and essence of reality are the same, then it would be impossible to ever hold that 'underdeveloped' countries submit to a particular logic of historical development. The basis of this illusion which conflates appearance with essence is a false empirical understanding of dependency. This understanding is anchored in an empirical conception of causality that categorically rejects the possibility that two different structures may ever exist in a contradictory unity. According to such an understanding, a unity is necessarily comprised of similar elements or structures that exist and evolve in an identitarian manner. This sort of thinking is fundamentally Hegelian, not Marxist. It would lead us to understand dependency – which is in fact the colonial relation itself – as a unity comprising, on the one hand, the coherent structure of capitalist production and, on the other hand, incoherent elements rather than a second coherent structure. These elements are [purportedly] moving towards forming a coherent structure which necessarily corresponds to the dominant and already coherent structure of capitalist production. In this scheme, the movement is one which progresses towards structural identification rather than structural differentiation. It thus suggests that a condition for dependency is the endurance of incoherent, broken elements within a framework of development which prevents them from uniting and fusing into a coherent structure.

Economic literature on 'underdevelopment', including Marxist works like Charles Bettelheim's valuable study, *India Independent*,[9] assumes that dependency exists and persists in colonised countries because the elements and sectors of production in these countries cannot cohere into a unity that amounts to a particular mode of production. This is where the notion that disequilibrium characterises an 'underdeveloped' economy comes from. In contemporary economic scholarship, the categorisation of production in 'underdeveloped' countries as essentially capitalist rests on viewing 'underdeveloped' production as [a set] of disjointed elements of a production structure that are not joined by the unity of the mode of production,[10] i.e. a coherent structural

9 Cf. Bettelheim 1962.

10 This definition of 'underdeveloped' production as disconnected elements rather than a coherent structure allows for the view that different structural sectors of production exist in 'underdeveloped' countries, such as capitalist, feudalist, pseudo-feudalist, traditional feudalist, primitive feudalist, pseudo-capitalist, etc. Charles Bettelheim attempted to go beyond this concept of 'underdevelopment' as an incoherent structure by refusing to look at it as an external frame encompassing different structures of production stuck together in a way that maintains their independence from one another. He instead identified a superposition [sic] of several different social structures. The term 'superposition' appears throughout his book (e.g. pp. 159, 125, 63, 45). Understood as signifying an organic interpenetration of the various social productions in a single 'backwards' country, this term affirms that numerous modes of production exist there. It does not therefore look at these various modes of production as self-sustaining and independent, but as basic components or elements that cohere with one another to constitute a distinct social mode of production with its own structural – and thus developmental – unity. This kind of interpenetration implied by the notion of 'superimposition' indicates the structural unity of the colonial mode of production.

whole. This contradiction is not a product of our thinking, but is borne by those who find it difficult to believe that social production in 'underdeveloped' countries might be a coherent production with its own distinct structural unity.

Conceiving of dependency in colonial production as the dependency of non-unified elements of production on a coherent structure of capitalist production renders this latter system of production the focal point that unifies these elements of production in our countries. In this scheme, the unity, in a relation of dependency on colonialism, lies between, on the one hand, incoherent elements of production and, on the other, a coherent (capitalist) production structure. If this were indeed the case, then dependency on colonialism would end when our social production attained coherence as a fully formed structure of capitalist production. In this scheme, the stage of dependency on colonialism would be but a transitory phase in the history of a capitalist mode of production. If this were so, colonialism would have created a material base in our countries for the development of capitalism, and independence would have been the historical realisation of possibilities for capitalist development that were created by colonialism itself (we mean 'material base' in the sense used by Marx in reference to the structural relation between forces and relations of production). This would lead us to conclude that capitalist development is a foundational and necessary stage through which colonised countries must pass.[11]

History – especially the post-WWII era – however, has shown the opposite to be true. While historical reality is crucial for verifying theory and gauging its scientific nature, let us bracket the question of whether this understanding of dependency (i.e. the colonial relation) is confirmed by historical reality to briefly highlight its weak theoretical basis. Even though this kind of thinking claims to be Marxist, it is in fact Hegelian in structure, which is why it is riddled with inner logical contradictions and does not reflect the historical reality it analyses. It is the Hegelian dialectic, in particular, which leads to a false view of the colonial relation. The Hegelian dialectic is a movement of identity rather than difference. It dissolves differences between everything it encompasses instead of revealing them. This dialectic therefore cannot see a unity in the movement of differentiation between two structures, a movement by which both develop within a single structural unity. As an idealist dialectic, it sees unity only in a single structure comprised of elements – not

11 'Marxist' thought passed through a phase where this kind of thinking dominated. Its contribution was the 'theory of national democracy'. However, both historical experience and what we have discussed thus far in the present study prove this theory to be lacking.

structures – and deems it impossible that they might differentiate and become uneven because all elements exist on a single level unified in thought, not reality. As a mode of thinking that dissolves the complex and differentiated unity into the identical unity of thought, the idealist essence of Hegelian dialectic makes it impossible to apprehend reality in its differentiated structural unity. The Marxist dialectic alone can reveal the structure of the colonial relation as a differentiated unity comprising two structures that continue to become differentiated while remaining bound in a structural unity with one another. Each structure as a whole passes through this movement of differentiation in its relation with the other, just as this movement operates within both as they continue to differentiate. The Marxist dialectic reveals this because it is at its base the movement of reality itself, which is a movement of differentiation and unevenness bound in the unity of contradictions.

Our view of the colonial relation as a relation of two structures within a contradictory unity draws on a particular tenet of Marxism-Leninism, namely the scientific-historical rule of the uneven development of contradictions within a structural unity. It should be clarified that this rule applies in principle to the form taken by the development of contradictions within a single structure, which, according to Marx and Lenin, is the capitalist social structure. We, on the other hand, use this rule as a theoretical method for analysing the contradiction between capitalist and colonial social structures which together comprise a whole. Our readers might question the validity of using this rule to analyse a relation between two structures, and whether it can truly reveal the particular logic of such a relation. We consider our previous analysis proof enough that it can. It is, however, of utmost importance on both theoretical and practical levels to demand further clarification on this issue. Some might misunderstand our use of this rule to understand the colonial relation. They might suppose that when invoking the law of uneven development, we are deeming the structural unity between capitalist and colonised or 'underdeveloped' countries to be like that which exists between two elements of one, rather than two, social structures. If this were the case, the unity that we are identifying between these countries would not exist on the level of the social structure's reality, but would, rather, be a construction of abstract thinking. The truth of the matter is that we did not come to see this unity between capitalist and colonial structures by way of a kind of thinking that strips each structure of its internal, conflicting contradictions of development and reduces each to either a simple, abstract whole or an element that plays a simple, abstract role in a contradiction. Such an approach to a contradictory whole is not only mistaken, but remote from reality, no matter how simple a given reality may appear. It is a fundamentally misleading, ideological view that distorts reality by concealing its complex essence. The Hegelian thinking which informs this approach reduces the contradiction's constituent parts to simple opposites that can never themselves embody a contradiction or contradictions. It is for this reason that Lenin described the Hegelian formulation of contradiction as a reflection of thought rather than the essence of reality. The colonial relation illustrates just how misleading this simplistic concept of contradiction is. Using it as a lens for analysing the complex contradiction between colonizing and colonised countries would make this contradiction appear as though it were simply between 'developed' and 'underdeveloped' countries. If the capitalist and colonial structures were stripped of their internal contradictions – which in each structure determine and are determined by the contradictions of the other structure – then the structural contradiction between the two would be a simple one between 'developed and underdeveloped'. In this formulation, the causes become invisible and the contradiction becomes metaphysical – a cryptic secret knowable only to God and to the masterfully deceptive guardians of bourgeois capitalist ideology.

We view the structural unity between capitalist and colonial structures as a unity comprising two differentiated structures where the movement of differentiation takes place in the framework of their differentiation as structures. This complex movement of differentiation is in fact a movement within a movement of differentiation. In other words, the defining framework of each structure and its development is defined by the framework of the unity of the two structures. The movement of differentiation within a unity is similarly complex because it is defined in its development within a universal structural framework by the movement of differentiation in the bounds of each structure. This complexity, which characterises the contradictory movement in the development of these structures' historical unity, reflects the layers of contradictions at play therein: there is the basic contradiction that encompasses the structural contradictions in each particular structure; then there is the complication presented by the existence of a dominant structure in the unity; and finally there is a dominant contradiction, which is the primary contradiction, in the unity of contradictions in each structure. This will become clearer to us in the coming analysis of the historical development of class contradictions particular to the colonial structure. The existence of a dominant structure in the unity of the two structures is the basis for conflict in their development, just as the existence of a dominant contradiction in the unity of the structure is the basis for conflict in the development of this structure's contradictions. Only Marxist thought captures the complex nature of the contradiction at the heart of historical reality, because the Marxist contradiction – unlike the Hegelian contradiction – is in its very nature complex. Examining the colonial relation through a Marxist lens is not a personal choice, but a necessarily imposed by historical reality on scientific thought.

In light of the complex Marxist contradiction, the colonial relation appears to us as the unity of two structures whose basis is a relation of domination. The unity here is not between two equal structures which exist on an even plane and a single structural level. Rather, it is a unity between capitalist and colonial structures in which the former dominates the latter in the process of development. As we saw in the first chapter of this study, the historical development of this unity is not a movement by which the two structures come to resemble one another, but, rather, a movement that differentiates the colonial structure from the capitalist structure in producing the former for the latter.

It is now urgent to emphasise that the basis of differentiation in this movement by which the unity of capitalist and colonial structures develops is the domination of the former over the latter. Were it not for this domination, historical development would not be a movement of structural differentiation. We should clarify that this movement of differentiation is in reality the conflict which transpires over the course of the unity's development. *This definition of the two structures' differentiation as unevenness in their structural unity is the theoretical basis for identifying colonialism as the cause of 'underdevelopment'.*

We must understand causality in this statement structurally, not mechanically. In other words, we must understand it to be a [capitalist] structure which, in the course of its development, produces another [colonial] structure that it dominates through incorporating it into itself in a structural unity that is the unity of historical development. Clarifying this 'structural causality' which drives colonial production towards capitalist production in the movement of its formation and becoming is our main challenge in the present study. The capitalist structure's domination over its colonial counterpart is actually the domination of capitalist production over colonial production – a correlation that should be clear to us. While this domination appears to be external at first glance, it is not. There is no separation between these structures, even if there is – or, more precisely, because there is – differentiation between them. In speaking of domination here, we do not mean the kind evident in the presence of colonial military bases in colonised or 'underdeveloped' countries, even though this presence is a plain, violent, and exceptionally dangerous form of colonial domination. The true domination that we mean to emphasise here is not merely the foundation for this and other forms of colonial domination, but what makes their existence possible. We are talking about the domination inherent in the very makeup and development of the colonial structure itself as a distinct social structure which cannot exist or persist except in unity with its capitalist counterpart. The domination of the capitalist structure in its unity with the colonial structure is manifested in the presence of a structural framework in which productive forces develop in a colonial mode of production; i.e. within colonial relations of production themselves as particular class relations. This is to say that *colonial domination over 'underdeveloped' countries inheres in the relations of production – which are colonial relations of production – in these countries. The true colonial domination is these countries' dependency on colonialism as represented in the social framework of colonial production. It exists first and foremost in the class relations particular to the colonial structures in these countries and not in a direct or active colonial presence, whether military or economic.*

For this reason, it is a mistake to speak about the end of colonialism in reference to the end of direct colonial presence. Similarly, the term 'neo-colonialism' currently tossed around in our political discourse is not accurate because it relies on and implies a false theoretical definition of colonialism. Colonialism is actually the colonial relation, and it does not necessarily disappear with the disappearance of colonising forces, the presence of which is but one of the violent forms taken by this relation. Indeed, the colonial relation continues to exist in many 'independent' 'underdeveloped' countries, which are actually dependent on colonialism in their 'independence'. The end of colonialism, to speak precisely, is linked to the end of colonial relations of production, which entails the transition from colonial production to socialist production enacted through a revolution for liberation, as we will see in what follows. The actual and permanent presence of colonialism is not direct, even though colonised countries experience it directly. Instead, colonialism exists through colonial relations of production, as a social framework for the historical development of forces of production in the colonial mode of production. In other words, it is embodied in the form in which classes, particular to the colonial social structure, exist. This means that colonialism's actual presence in 'underdeveloped' colonised countries is not direct, even when they are subjected to direct colonial rule. This is because colonialism exists not in itself, but in its effect or production. To restate an earlier argument, it exists in the social structure that it produces, a structure that comes to be distinct through the process of its development. The structure's particularity lies in its dependency on colonialism, not its independence from colonialism. This is the point that we meant to clarify in discussing the structural causality linking colonialism and 'underdevelopment'. This distinct relation of causality is the truth of the colonial relation, which we have not yet finished analysing. Let us now consider this relation in light of our definition of the colonial social structure as a particular class structure.

In performing a class analysis of the colonial structure, the theoretical difficulty does not only consist in the colonial structure's distinctiveness and particularity in relation to the capitalist structure but also in its determined relation with the Marxist thought analysing it. Marxist thought, seemingly wanting in this analysis, exists in tension with the colonial structure. The problem is that the scheme in Marxist thought for analysing class structure was created through analysis of the capitalist structure. Yet, we must rely on this theoretical scheme to analyse the colonial structure as a class structure, albeit one that exists in a structural relationship with the capitalist structure. The differentiation between the two structures in the movement of their development as a unity means that this theoretical scheme created for analysing the capitalist structure is absolutely incommensurable with the colonial class structure. The difficulty lies in the contradiction between the exigency with which this theoretical scheme presents itself as an instrument of class analysis and the incommensurability between it and colonial class reality. It is as though Marxist thought, while the only instrument for class analysis, is itself an obstacle to performing the necessary analysis. The truth, however, is that the tension we see between Marxist thought and colonial reality is necessarily concomitant with the process of knowledge production itself, which is always a dialectical movement that enriches thought by unveiling reality.

We can see this process at work in our analysis of the colonial social structure. This structure's basic characteristic is the lack of differentiation between the social classes which constitute it. For example, there is no class barrier dividing the bourgeoisie from the proletariat because the borders between these two main classes are not clearly marked. The main reason for the lack of class differentiation lies in the historical conditions for these classes' formation in colonised countries, which are also the conditions for the formation of the colonial structure itself. Their lack of differentiation is determined as a form of their historical development during their formation, a topic which we have already broached. For example, the colonial bourgeoisie – by which we mean the class mistakenly called the 'national' bourgeoisie – was and still is determined by its historical formation as a mercantile bourgeoisie that was consumed by its economic activity in the movement of import and export, equipping colonial industry with raw materials and selling its products. The development of this bourgeoisie was structured by the global colonial division of labour. Its trajectory of development from a mercantile to financial bourgeoisie, without passing through an industrial phase, distinguishes this class from the colonialist bourgeoisie. The role of the development of industry – if we can speak of actual industry in these countries – was as a result taken up by a faction of the petite bourgeoisie that cannot break out of its class boundaries in the constrictive framework of colonial production. This class condition was bound to impact the working class's existence and becoming. Since the colonial bourgeoisie's development and becoming did not pass through an industrial phase – because of the colonial relation itself – the possibility of differentiation in the working class over the course of its becoming was suppressed. Perhaps it is more accurate to say that there was a very narrow margin for such differentiation whereby it was difficult for the working class to form as an independent, complete entity that would confront, through its differentiation as a class, this productive sector of an otherwise basically unproductive petite bourgeoisie.

This brings us to a basic point about the undifferentiated class structure that characterises the colonial social structure: *The distinct historical form in which the confrontation of the working class [with the petite bourgeoisie] unfolded through its becoming as a class is the root for the lack of class differentiation in the colonial structure. The fact that the colonial bourgeoisie was determined as a mercantile-financial class represented by the colonizing bourgeoisie gave rise to a specific – if not anomalous – class condition whereby the working class confronted the productive sector of the petite bourgeoisie rather than the capitalist bourgeoisie as occurred in the West, given that the latter class cannot exist in colonial society.* The colonial relation – as a relation of domination of capitalist, and thereby metropolitan, production over colonial production – determined the structure of colonial production in such a way that it came to restrain and indeed paralyse the movement of class differentiation rather than free it. In other words, the framework in which class differentiation operates in colonial societies necessarily embeds the development of classes in a structure of non-differentiation. This is because the forces of production in colonial production are necessarily dependent on the development of forces of production in capitalist production.

From the moment that colonial relations of production took shape as a framework for development, they were determined in a particular way that absolutely prevented them from developing so as to create the conditions for the sort of class differentiation we see in the capitalist West. The development of agriculture through colonial relations, which directed it towards capitalist production as well as import and export, prevented these conditions from materialising. In drawing this conclusion, we are merely applying a general Marxist law concerning the historical development of social structures. This is the law, as stated in the text we cited earlier, of the existence of a correspondence between relations of production [on one hand] and the degree of the development of the forces of production in a given mode of production on the other. Based on this law, we can say that the development of forces of production in colonial societies can never resemble the development of forces of production in capitalist societies, which is to say that they cannot develop in a way that would bring about the industrial revolution necessary to free them. In other words, the forces of production can only be freed through shattering the colonial framework by the distinct form of class struggle waged in the colonial social structure. Before delving into our discussion of this particular form of class conflict, we must define classes within the structure of colonial relations of production, or, in other words, how they exist as classes.

When we define the colonial framework as an undifferentiated structure, we are by no means denying that there are blatant inequalities between the various sectors of colonial society, especially between the colonial bourgeoisie and the rest of the labouring popular classes. These inequalities do not necessarily constitute class differentiation, even if they seem more extreme than class inequalities in capitalist society, where there is class differentiation. Generally speaking, the contrast visible in colonial societies such as India and Indonesia between extraordinary poverty, on the one hand, and opulent mansions with flashy cars and servants, on the other, is not found in capitalist societies. This is because, as Marx says, class differentiation between social classes is not determined by consumption, but by the social production that qualitatively and quantitatively determines social consumption. The class structure of colonial society is therefore determined on the level of colonial production and within its structural framework. As we know, basic production in colonial societies is fundamentally agricultural-mercantile. Its development, moreover, always follows colonial capitalist production, and its dependency on this production is evident in its lacking an industrial phase. As a mercantile-financial class, the colonial bourgeoisie was thus a consumer bourgeoisie that represents its colonialist counterpart in colonial society. Because it was impossible for the colonial bourgeoisie to be an active, independent class, it was determined as a distinct class only by virtue of its representational function. Its survival in colonial society is tied to the persistence of the conditions that render its formation as an independent class, which is to say a productive bourgeoisie, impossible. This means that the colonial bourgeoisie is only a class insofar as it represents another class. This impossibility, a result of the colonial relation, furnishes the structural basis for the lack of class differentiation in the colonial social structure. This non-differentiation is itself the basis for such brazen differences between the various factions of colonial society. Seemingly self-contradictory, this statement is sound because the sort of extreme differences we see in a colonial society are on the level of consumption alone (meaning that they are differences between each faction's ability to consume) and not production. Indeed, the acute nature of these differences is a product of the colonial bourgeoisie's makeup as a class that consumes rather than produces.

Colonial production lacks an industrial phase. As a result, land generally constitutes the fundamental means of production in colonial society. This means that agrarian production is dominant over industrial production. Despite this dominance, we cannot speak of 'feudal' relations of production between peasants and agricultural proprietors due to the fact that all agricultural production (especially its 'developed' sectors) mediated by the colonial relation is fundamentally directed towards export, i.e. towards colonial capitalist production. Because agricultural production develops within the bounds of the colonial relation, agrarian proprietors do not constitute a distinct feudal class of the bourgeoisie (as was the case in the West, for example) but, rather, comprise a sector of the colonial bourgeoisie. That is to say, they are a faction of the mercantile-financial bourgeoisie that we introduced in the first chapter of this study. The distinct nature of the structure of colonial production appears to us clearly in the fact that peasants (especially the agricultural workers) bear the burden of exploitation, indeed overexploitation, more so than any other social class. Because colonial production developed within the colonial relation and was directed fundamentally towards export, colonialism is the fundamental exploitative force in colonial society. The exploitative relation between [colonial society's] peasants and colonialism is indirect because it operates through the latter's representative in colonial society, namely the various factions of the colonial bourgeoisie.

The basis of class unity of the different factions of the colonial bourgeoisie (mercantile, financial, and agrarian) resides in these factions' representation of the colonialist bourgeoisie. Class cohesion is therefore essential among these factions – a segment of which may be simultaneously mercantile, financial, agrarian, and even industrial. If a contradiction were to arise between any of them, it would be secondary and ephemeral at best because the basis of their class unity is the representative relation linking each to the colonialist bourgeoisie. Having been determined as a representative or 'parasitic' class, it is impossible on a structural level for the colonial bourgeoisie to ever become a productive class. The primary class confrontation [in colonial society], moreover, is between this class and the peasants. If land is the basic means of production in colonial society, then peasants must be the its basic productive force. Within the bounds of colonial agricultural production, peasants directly confront this class in their production, which is the site of their exploitation by the colonial bourgeoisie's agricultural faction and thus the entire class in its unity. This class confrontation, however, is in fact only a manifestation of the real, structural confrontation between the peasants and colonialism, the latter of which is represented by the colonial bourgeoisie. In other words, peasants are actually confronting colonialism through their social production when they confront the colonial bourgeoisie, even if this confrontation does not appear to their consciousness as such. This structural class reality will appear to the peasants of colonial society only through class struggle which indeed determines their consciousness as distinct class consciousness, i.e. a consciousness of national liberation.

We have yet to analyse the trajectory of class becoming for the different classes of colonial society. Our analysis has thus far focused more on class existence rather than class becoming. In the next section, we will analyse the development of colonial society's class structure through class struggle, which is the force that unifies its trajectory of becoming.

The relations of production specific to the colonial mode of production have begun to reveal themselves [at the time of writing]. Indeed, the class confrontations between the peasants and colonial bourgeoisie as well as that between the working class and petite bourgeoisie (the latter being the productive faction of an otherwise unproductive class) have brought the outline of the colonial class structure into sharp relief. We must note here that the confrontation between the peasants and colonial bourgeoisie in the context of agricultural production is not separate or independent from the confrontation between the workers and petite bourgeoisie in the context of 'small-scale' consumer industry. It must not be forgotten that when we delineate these class contradictions, we are defining them within the unity of the social structure encompassing them. They are not, therefore, two independent class contradictions running parallel to each other. To define them as such would be to fall into the very trap of structural dualism that we previously rejected. It would also make it impossible to properly comprehend the reason for the lack of class differentiation in the colonial [social] structure. It is impossible for these two contradictions to exist in separation because confrontation between the workers and petite bourgeoisie, for example, is possible in this 'unnatural' form only because the colonial bourgeoisie is an unproductive class that represents a productive one [the colonialist bourgeoisie]. The colonial bourgeoisie's 'parasitic' or representational nature is thus what defines the contradiction between the workers and petite bourgeoisie. It also determines whether the class contradiction between the colonial bourgeoisie and the peasants is feudal or capitalist in nature.

To dispel any illusions that might come from misunderstanding what we are saying here, we want to stress a fundamental point about the colonial class structure, namely the class dominance of the colonial bourgeoisie – due to its representation of the colonialist bourgeoisie – over colonial society. Class dominance by the colonial bourgeoisie leads to a lack of class differentiation in colonial society, a lack which distinguishes it structurally from its capitalist counterpart. Due to its class dominance and representation of colonialism, the unproductive consumer bourgeoisie exists in a specific relation of exploitation with the rest of the exploited classes.[12] This relation in turn imposes a development

12 Unlike the productive nature of the colonialist bourgeoisie's consumption.

structure on these exploited classes that is necessarily lacking in class differentiation. The dominance of colonial society's unproductive class situates its social classes in a structure where productive class relations are determined as undifferentiated class relations. This is why the exploited classes – namely the workers, peasants, and petite bourgeoisie – are even less differentiated. This is due to the fact that the class relations of exploitation linking these classes to the ruling class (the colonial bourgeoisie) are not in their essence relations of direct exploitation actualised in the framework of production. Having never passed through the industrial phase, the relations of exploitation in [colonial] production remain indirect because colonialism is the active exploitative force. The colonial bourgeoisie exists as a class merely to bring the process of colonial exploitation into effect. The structural reason for the impossibility of class differentiation developing between the exploited classes lies in the indirect nature of social exploitation (as enacted by the colonial bourgeoisie's class dominance) in colonial production. *The lack of class differentiation between classes in colonial society is prior to the existence of the classes themselves and inheres in the social structure* [*of colonial society*]. This means that the structural framework for the development of classes in colonial society necessitates its undifferentiated form.

It is thus theoretically and scientifically unsound to speak about class formation at all in this society, if in using the term 'class formation' we mean the differentiated development of classes. The very structure of colonial production prohibits the movement of class differentiation, meaning that we may never speak of a class-in-formation in the framework of colonial society. Characterised essentially by a lack of class differentiation, the undifferentiated colonial social structure frames the development of classes in colonial society, which, as a result, is overtaken by stagnation and repetition. In other words, its movement is not the progressive or ascendant movement of capitalist development. Rather, it is a closed, stagnant, and repetitive movement that necessarily inhibits the formation of differentiated classes. Herein lies the true meaning of 'the vicious cycle of underdevelopment'. It is precisely the undifferentiated structural framework of colonial production, which is the continual production of colonial relations, that bourgeois economic literature attempts to hide in speaking of this 'vicious cycle'.

Class differentiation takes shape through the progressive development of production as it came to be in the capitalist West. Because colonial production develops in the strictures of a relation of dependency that connects it to capitalist production on a structural level – and thus in a circular, repetitive form that is anything but ascendant – class differentiation cannot possibly emerge in its relations of production. In contrast to capitalist production, the closed nature of colonial production structures the development of classes within it in a way that precludes their differentiation. In other words, this impossibility is embedded in the structure of colonial production itself. This is readily evident, for example, in the fact that the migration of peasants in colonial societies to urban centres seldom brings about a radical class transformation whereby one differentiated class becomes another, as in the transformation of a peasant class into a working class. The reason for this is the absence of true industry, in the capitalist sense of the word. If the peasant were to become a worker in a colonial society – a rare occurrence indeed – it would occur in the framework of small-scale consumer craft industry. In such a framework, it is difficult for radical class transformation to occur on the levels of [class] existence and consciousness. Although embedded in a new class formation, peasants in colonial society [who have migrated to cities] nonetheless preserve most of their class connections. This class thus retains its previous consciousness in perceiving its new existence. The ease with which peasants transition from one class existence to another without ever experiencing a rupture in their class transformation can be traced to the structure of the working class as it is produced through small-scale consumer industry.

In Lebanon, for example, the difference between peasant and worker is very difficult to define in terms of class existence and consciousness. This is because production itself does not allow for such definition [to come about] in the general structure of social production. The [Lebanese] worker returns to his village at every opportunity, for holidays, vacations, and funerals. In this way, his village becomes his centre of gravity and exerts a pull over him stronger than that of the city. Ultimately, he longs for the land he had left and demands to be buried there, home to his ancestors. We can therefore say that the worker is a peasant whose social transformation into a worker has failed due to the colonial nature of the social structure [in which he exists] that absolutely precludes the process of social transformation from reaching its end. His transformation cannot take place because it is impossible for this structure to reach the industrial phase. Capitalist production is capable of severing the connection by which a worker may return to his previous class state. For this reason, the social phenomena born of the worker's constant longing for his village and land that we find in colonial societies are rarely found in a Western capitalist society, because this longing reflects the possibility that he may in fact return to the class existence out of which he transformed.

In other words, the class transition of peasants from one differentiated class to another, i.e. from his village and land to the city and factory, that transpires in a colonial society is incommensurable with this transition in a capitalist society, where it is truly a transformation. The 'freedom' to switch classes is a defining characteristic of the relations of colonial production. The worker as we find him in a colonial society may simultaneously be a peasant, just as he may be a seller of consumer goods in his spare time, or, in other words, a petit bourgeois. In the colonial social structure, there is no gravitational pull of class that sorts individuals and firmly establishes them within stable class boundaries. This is due to the colonial makeup of production [in these societies], i.e. its dependency on capitalist production. The distinguishing feature of the colonial social structure *as* an undifferentiated class structure reveals itself in sharp relief through the impossibility of the class transformation of peasants into workers as a result of the productive process In this undifferentiated class structure, therefore, class consciousness is closer to a class illusion than class consciousness. The loss of what we referred to above as the gravitational pull of class (a result of the lack of defined, differentiated classes) leads the individual – and also the class – in this society to hope to climb up a step in the social ladder. In hoping to break through the bounds of his class, he does not seek to break the framework of his society's class structure, but to ascend into the upper class with which he and his class are in contradiction and conflict. The presence of this hope in consciousness is a sign of the belief that such an ascension is possible. Even though this possibility is illusory and imaginative, its mere appearance to the consciousness of he who experiences it as real and not imaginary gives class consciousness an ideological form, i.e. an illusory form that necessarily makes for non-revolutionary political practice.

In this state of being, class consciousness does not perceive class struggle as a necessity. Instead, it aims for class substitution. There is a fundamental difference between class conflict and class substitution, even if the first necessarily entails one class replacing another [at the helm of] political power. However, the wresting of this power from the ruling class (such as the bourgeoisie) to place it in the grasp of the exploited class (such as the proletariat) takes place through a class struggle that necessarily culminates in the destruction of the existing social structure, say that of capitalist relations of production, and transition to a different one, say socialist mode of production.

In other words, the violence of class struggle that develops within a specific social structure peaks when it breaks the existing social framework and transitions to another one. Meanwhile, class substitution occurs within the bounds of the social structure itself without bringing about a structural change in the social mode of production. We see examples of this in colonised countries that have not brought their liberation revolution to its culmination, despite having achieved 'political independence', whereby the settler colonialist bourgeoisie is replaced by the colonial bourgeoisie, the class often referred to as the 'national' bourgeoisie. This substitution of the colonialist capitalist bourgeoisie by the colonial bourgeoisie at the level of political power does not itself change the social structure of production into something other than colonial production. Rather than changing the social structure itself, this substitution constitutes a change within a persistent social structure. In the best of circumstances, this class substitution brings about a transition from dependent dependence, so to speak, to 'dependent independence'. It is not therefore a transition from either one social structure to another or one mode of production to another. Lebanon illustrates this clearly.

In saying this, we are not at all denying the importance of what is called 'political independence', even if this expression is scientifically imprecise. What we want to highlight here is that this 'independence' does not necessarily entail a transition from one mode of production to another. For the most part, this 'independence' is achieved within the framework of the colonial mode of production itself and represents an actualisation of potential development inherent within that framework. So long as the structure of colonial production remains in place, it is difficult for us to speak of independence and, moreover, impossible to speak of a revolution of liberation. We have already seen how the concept of 'class substitution' helps us understand (with something of the scientific precision that we desperately need to understand our contemporary history) what happens in colonised countries upon their achievement of 'independence'. Indeed, this concept helps us comprehend the relation of substitution and representation between the petite bourgeoisie and colonial bourgeoisie in several countries that attempted to liberate themselves from colonialism, such as Algeria and Egypt.

So as not to get ahead of ourselves, suffice it here to say that the petite bourgeoisie's replacement[13] of the colonial bourgeoisie as a ruling class does not amount to a change of social structure, i.e. to a transition from one structure of production to another (e.g. socialist production). For the most part, the phenomenon of class substitution is specific to colonial societies and unknown in Western capitalist societies, where the replacement of one class by another occurs through intense class struggle that always leads to a radical structural

13 Here, we want to point out to the reader that class substitution should not be understood in a mechanical sense. The movement of displacement is actually the movement of development, and indeed of formation for the class that replaces the other class. It is possible for new contradictions to be produced through class substitution that were not present in the social structure before this substitution occurred. The existence of these new contradictions, however, does not radically influence the social structure. In other words, it does not bring about the sort of revolutionary change that transpires through the transition to a new social structure. They are therefore new contradictions within the existing social structure itself. This is especially clear in the petite bourgeoisie's replacement of the colonial bourgeoisie as a ruling class, a process that occurred in Egypt, for example. We will return to this point later.

change in the mode of social production itself. For example, the bourgeoisie's replacement of the feudal nobility as the ruling class led to a revolutionary social transformation in the West that constituted a transition from a feudal mode of production to a capitalist mode of production.

As for colonial societies, it is rare that class substitution takes the shape of clear, intense class conflict due to the nature of their social structure, which lacks class differentiation. In other words, it is due to the colonial relation itself. In our countries, as we have seen, colonialism produced a particular social structure of classes. Through our political struggle, we have begun to comprehend the difficulty – but not impossibility – of transcending this structure. The presence of class substitution as a form of class struggle is proof that this non-differentiated social structure is distinct from its capitalist counterpart. It is as though the colonial social structure harbours internal and promising possibilities for development to the point of eliminating the necessity for a transition to another social structure. Indeed, the persistence of this non-differentiated structure after 'independence' as a framework for development seems to signal that such development is possible. But the repetitive form of this development, however, indicates otherwise, that it is historically necessary to break out of it. The repetitive form of development apparent in the 'vicious cycle of underdevelopment' creates the illusion that the colonial structures harbours a rich array of possibilities for development. There is an element of continuity in the repetitive [cycle] of [colonial] development. That is absent in the upward development of capitalism as illustrated by the latter's crises. The difficulty in transcending the colonial structure is rooted in this force of continuity, hidden in the movement of the structure's repetitive development. To transcend the colonial structure, the colonial relation must be severed to thereby free the movement of historical development.

There is no doubt that class substitution as a form of class struggle in the undifferentiated class structure of colonial society can potentially – in certain circumstances – create tension between the classes. This tension, however, rarely generates a political struggle. By political struggle, we are referring to class struggle seeking a radical – and indeed revolutionary – transformation of the social structure that does not preserve this structure. The tension in the process of class substitution breeds feelings of bitterness among the classes, or among particular factions of the displaced class. That is to say, it produces a 'psychological' struggle that can never be said to have a political meaning even if it erupts in violence and open rebellion. To a certain extent, this clarifies why 'political' practice in most 'Third World' countries – despite its overtly violent character – is incapable of achieving any effective change to the social structure, which is to say a 'structural mutation', or, as [Abdallah] al-ʿAlayli describes it, a structural 'shock'.[14] The so-called 'political' movements in India, Pakistan, and the Middle East illustrate this plainly. Throughout the 'social explosions' in these countries, their respective social structures remain in place, as these 'explosions' prove incapable of breaking these structures' frameworks to free the forces of production within them. The fact of the matter is that the lack of 'political' stability which differentiates these countries from the politically stable countries of the capitalist West strangely corresponds with the persistent stability of their socio-political structures. This stability of structure, or rather the perseverance of this stability, is in fact a condition for the lack of 'political' stability [in 'Third World' countries]. Put more precisely, it may be said that the lack of 'political' stability is the way in which class substitution is expressed historically, through class practice, in a non-differentiated class structure. The seemingly daily 'revolutions' (military coups) that have become part and parcel of political folklore in these 'Third World' countries are nothing but outbursts. When the dust settles, the social structure turns out to have remained intact and stable throughout.

We would like to make a remark on this topic before moving on. Stability of the social structure, which is a condition for the lack of so-called 'political' stability in colonial societies, differs absolutely from the structural stability of Western capitalist societies. In the capitalist West, structural stability is actually a direct result of the structure's dynamism or, more precisely, of the particular kind of social dialectic that exists between differentiated classes. As for the stability of structure in colonial societies, it is [conversely] a result of the *paralysis of the social dialectic* that occurs among undifferentiated classes. At the same time, this paralysis necessarily results in a persistently undifferentiated class structure. The non-differentiation of social classes in colonial societies is thus at once the cause and effect of this paralysis. The historical trajectory of these societies become as a result ambiguous. In order to highlight the difference between colonial and Western-capitalist structures, we should perhaps reserve the use of the word 'fixedness' to exclusively describe the former and the word 'stability' to exclusively describe the latter.

We will now turn to investigating the significance of this ambiguity, which is a result of the lack of differentiation between the social classes, in the historical trajectory of colonial societies. It is as though this lack of differentiation suspends, so to speak, these societies' becoming. It ostensibly absolves them from having to subscribe to a necessary logic of [transformation] and instead

14 Editor's note: Abdallah al-ʿAlayli was a prominent twentieth-century Arabo-Islamic reformer sympathetic to socialism.

opens (or appears to open) a multiplicity of choices [for becoming]. This false understanding of their historical movement as restrained and lacking necessity informs the widespread claim that these societies have a 'choice' between socialism and capitalism, i.e. between 'non-capitalist' and capitalist paths of development. [For those who believe this,] it is as though history, upon reaching colonial societies, loses all rationality and is determined instead by a personal or subjective decision. The trajectory of these societies is thus understood in contrast to rational [capitalist] societies as the outcome of a free choice made by someone, a sovereign individual perhaps, in isolation from any historical necessity or objective laws. In this view, such necessity and laws do not apply to these societies because they do not develop according to objective reason.

This strange way of looking at history, and at the history of colonial societies, in particular, negates history by reducing it to a subjective choice. It is unclear as to how history is objective in capitalist societies and subjective in colonial ones. The truth is that there is a logical contradiction in this way of looking at history, and it is based on a mistaken understanding of the movement of historical development in colonial societies. In this view, the decision of the ruler (e.g. Nasser, Ben Bella, Sékou Touré, Castro) constitutes the determining force of history. A country will develop into a capitalist country, according to this logic, if the ruler puts his country on the path of capitalist development. It will alternatively develop into a socialist country if he put is on the path of non-capitalist development. It is as if achieving socialism and severing ties with colonialism are contingent on a decision taken by the ruler. The essential condition for the socialist transformation of colonial society is therefore the transformation of the individual leader into a socialist who believes that socialism is the horizon of historical development in his country. The fact that Cuba turned towards socialism is thus attributed to Castro's desire for it to do so. As for Algeria, it did not take this direction because Ben Bella did not want it for his country. We do not say so out of exaggeration or sarcasm. This is the view of many who see the later revolutionary experiences of colonial countries in this light.

Debating this topic is not our concern, as many books may be cited to prove that this is the case. Rather, our concern is to reveal the basis for this mistaken understanding of the movement of history in colonial societies. At the core of such a view is an idealism that situates history in a social structure's superstructure and separates historical movement from class development (i.e. the material basis of the social structure), thereby reducing it to the subjective will of the individual or faction in power. The distinctiveness of the colonial structure as a structure of undifferentiated classes is what allows this mistaken logic to take hold. When held against the capitalist structure, a structure of clear class differentiation, the colonial structure appears as though it is moving towards formation and completion [to become like its capitalist progenitor], and not as though it is already formed and completed. The existence of the colonial structure in a state of potential formation and completion renders it historically similar to the capitalist structure – something we have already rejected. Such a [perceived] state hollows its development from the precise, rational logic governing the development of the capitalist structure and thereby opens it up to structural possibilities that are impossible for the capitalist structure to open up to. This is because the logic of formation [of a social structure] – as we have already mentioned – completely differs from the logic of its development, which is the movement of an already formed structure.

It follows that the horizon of possibility is open within the logic of formation and closed in the face of the logic of development. This is where the idea of 'freedom of choice' in colonial societies' development comes from, as we see it in the bad political literature on these societies. The contradiction here is clear: this 'freedom of choice' is possible only if we look at this structure as if it were in the process of formation. However, looking at it this way is also not possible unless we take its historical development to be identical to that of an already-formed capitalist structure, as this would be the standard for development and definition as a structure in formation. How then could there be such 'freedom of choice', i.e. the possibility of [the colonial social structure] developing towards a non-capitalist horizon,[15] if the condition for its existence is its resemblance to the capitalist structure? The truth is that if this 'freedom of choice' theory and the voluntary view of history it is based on tells us anything at all, it is that the colonial structure and the laws which govern its development are sorely misunderstood. Indeed, there appears to be total ignorance of the reality of the colonial relation. This strange view of Marxism is most likely not the res-

15 The expression 'non-capitalist development' is not a scientific expression. This is because it does not positively define the social structure to which it alludes. Rather, it is a negative definition that does not reveal the reality of the structure it defines. In other words, it defines the structure by what it cannot become rather than what it is in itself. When we say, for example, that Egypt – or Algeria or Syria – has taken the course of 'non-capitalist development', we are defining their development negatively, stating that it is not capitalist in nature. While this is true, we are leaving the nature of this 'non-capitalist' social development undefined. As a term, 'non-capitalist development' is not therefore identical to the term 'socialist development', even if they resonate this way for many people. The phrase 'non-capitalist development' is a sign of the incapacity of 'theoretical' thought to define the structure of social production in particular countries. It is clear in this expression, specifically, that this [still undefined] productive structure is not capitalist, just as it is not a socialist. More than anything else, our study is an attempt to provide a positive definition for this structure of social production.

ult of a serious theoretical effort, even if it has an implicitly 'theoretical' basis. More than anything, it is an ideological view. Moreover, it necessarily excludes 'Third World' countries from the movement of history, the latter becoming confined to the existential confrontation between the two major global powers, namely the capitalist and socialist 'camps'. The 'Third World' exists outside of this primary historical contradiction, isolated from the movement generated by the engine of history constituted by the confrontation between these two camps. This actual isolation from the movement of history is what makes it seem as though [the Third World's] has not committed path, but subject to [whimsical] 'freedom of choice'.

We will not delve any further into a debate that takes us away from our topic. Our concern in this study is to analytically approach the ambiguity that characterises the historical trajectory of colonial societies in light of their specific class relations. The truth is that this ambiguity is only apparent, not real. This is because the non-differentiation between social classes works in the economic and political favour of a particular class in colonial society, namely the petite bourgeoisie. Because it straddles the bourgeoisie and the working class, the petite bourgeoisie always wavers between the two without ever settling in one position. This constant instability on both political and economic fronts determines its social position as a 'wavering' class that has no clear or determined political principles.

This is generally true of both the 'underdeveloped' and 'developed' petite bourgeoisie. However, what distinguishes the petite bourgeoisie in a capitalist society from its counterpart in a colonial society is that in the former, the petit bourgeoisie is determined as a class by the movement of differentiation between the bourgeoisie and proletariat. In the latter however, it is the outcome of the movement of non-differentiation between social classes. Put more precisely, the petite bourgeoisie in a capitalist society is the left-over or by-product of the central social movement of confrontation between society's formative classes, namely the bourgeoisie and proletariat. This movement thus ejects the petite bourgeoisie from history, in which it exists only as a parasitic outgrowth (excrescence). In this sense, it is an anomaly in the theoretical existence of a capitalist society. From this perspective, Marx was right in his analysis of capitalist society to put forth the concept of capitalism as an apt tool for analysing the reality of capitalist society. The petite bourgeoisie in the West is indeed a disruptive, parasitic entity that muddles the theoretical clarity of capitalism as a concept, complicating it without benefit and preventing the concept from cohering.

As for the petite bourgeoisie in colonial society, it is nothing less than the centrepoint of history's movement. This is because it is the most differentiated class in a social structure lacking class differentiation. The historical movement of class structure [in colonial societies] resembles axial rotation, and the petite bourgeoisie is the axis around which it revolves. All other class positions in this social structure are determined in relation to this fundamental axis. In this scheme, the class divergence separating the bourgeoisie and the proletariat is revealed to be so great that it is difficult for the two classes to ever confront one another in serious class conflict while conscious of the class significance of such a conflict. This is the opposite of what we see in the capitalist West, for example. The colonial nature of the bourgeoisie [in colonial society] turns the class confrontation with the proletariat, on the level of production, into a confrontation with the productive sector of the petite bourgeoisie. This is an inverse image of the historical social structure presented by the West: In colonial society, the parasitic class is the bourgeoisie – not the petite bourgeoisie. This bourgeoisie is a direct outcome (or, more precisely a nearly direct outcome) of the colonialist bourgeoisie, and is, therefore, from the moment of its emergence and by virtue of its emergence, afflicted with a structural incapacity that absolutely prevents it from becoming a leading force of history that it is in the West.

We must take this opportunity to emphasise that the formation of a working class in colonial society into a proletariat i.e. as a revolutionary independent class aware of its class existence, is a historically particular process. In a capitalist society, the formation of the working class as a revolutionary class is actualised through an intense class struggle against the ruling bourgeoisie; here the class contradiction is clear and apparent, as is the process of its development. In colonial society, on the other hand, the class contradiction between the bourgeoisie and the working class is a complicated contradiction, determined by another contradiction with the petite bourgeoisie. On the level of social production, the fact that there is a confrontation between the working class and the petite bourgeoisie does not negate that a fundamental contradiction exists between the working class and the colonial bourgeoisie. On the contrary, this latter contradiction is fundamental because it hinders the development of the working class and foils its formation. It also crucially determines the contradiction between the working class and the petite bourgeoisie. When the working class confronts the petite bourgeoisie in the movement of social production and its own class becoming, it must also necessarily confront the colonial bourgeoisie which as stated hinders the working class's formation. In this light, the class contradiction in capitalist society appears to be far simpler than the class contradiction in colonial society. Through its direct confrontation with the petite bourgeoisie in the context of production, the working class [in colonial society] finds that its class conflict with the colonial bourgeoisie, and thus with colonialism itself, is necessary. Through its class becoming, the struggle of the working class in the sphere of production is revealed to us as a struggle for its very existence as a class, i.e. as a struggle to free up the historical process of its own class formation. Herein lies the distinction of the [class] contradiction in colonial society.

From a class perspective, the historical becoming of colonial societies is distinguished less so by the non-differentiation [per se] between social classes that we see in the colonial structure than it does by the distinct character of this non-differentiation. What sets the non-differentiation endemic to the colonial class structure apart from any other kind of non-differentiation is the fact that it is the historical outcome of the sharp class differentiation in the capitalist social structure. The particular movement of class differentiation in the colonial social structure emerged and developed in the wake of this structure's subjection to colonial domination, which catalysed this movement. There is no doubt that the rupture inflicted by Western capitalism's colonial development was the decisive factor that pushed forward the movement of class differentiation in colonial societies. However, the existence of the colonial relation – as one of domination between two differentiated social structures – necessarily determined this class movement to be non-differentiation. This relation continues to determine the form of 'peaceful coexistence' that exists between capitalist and colonial societies today. It follows that the non-differentiation of classes in colonial societies is what constitutes the structural framework for the actualisation of the movement of class differentiation.

In other words, so long as the colonial relation remains in place, the differentiation of classes in the colonial structure cannot be actualised due to the framework of this class structure, which is one of non-differentiation. We thus find ourselves before two absolutely inseparable movements that are in fact two sides of a single, complicated process, namely that of the historical process of totalisation whereby each movement is unified by contradictory structures of differentiation. Each structure is a fundamental condition for the other's existence. Their relationship is causal and determined within a framework of domination. The particular kind of causality linking them prevents the relation uniting them from ever being superposed externally. The relation between the capitalist and colonial structures, as we have said, is one of universalisation that persists through the movement of differentiation. Yet it is also a relation of differentiation that persists through the movement of universalisation. This is what we have attempted to understand through fleshing out the concept of structural causality. It is also what compelled us to consider the social production in 'underdeveloped' countries as distinct production that differs from capitalist production in terms of both structure and development.[16]

16 Whoever wants to consider social production in what we have called 'colonial societies'

In this chapter, we have attempted to define the nature of the productive class relations specific to the colonial mode of production. We have yet to analyse the historical development of these relations, which would be to define the trajectories of the various classes in colonial society with an eye to the structural unity of their relations. A definition of the colonial class structure must be followed by a definition of the logic of its historical becoming. In other words, we must now turn to defining the conditions of possibility for socialist revolution in the colonial structure, beginning with an attempt to define the development of its distinct class contradictions. This is what we will attempt in the third part of this study.

(i.e. in 'underdeveloped countries') to be capitalist production that is structurally analogous to social production in Western countries has forgotten the following: the basic characteristic of capitalist production that sets it apart from all prior forms of social production is its tendency, as Lenin put it, towards limitless expansion. The necessity of capitalism's colonial phase is rooted in this distinctive internal logic of the development of capitalist production. Colonialism is inherent in the development of capitalist production. Nothing of the sort can be said about colonial production. What kind of logic could ever lead us to judge this production to be capitalist? Is it not enough to note the impossibility of colonial production ever attaining a capitalist phase of development? This alone should urge us to look at colonial production as distinct from capitalist production both in its structure and development.

CHAPTER 5

On the Sectarian State

Book Title:
On the Sectarian State
Beirut: Dar al-Farabi, 3rd edition, 2003. (First published in 1986).

Chapter 5: The Question of History

Section 8: Materialist Thought and the Sectarian Question

The problem is clearly the following: can we view sectarianism through the lens of class analysis? Are the specific conceptual and theoretical tools of materialist thought capable of producing a concrete knowledge of a concrete situation known in Lebanon as 'sectarianism'? In producing such knowledge, it is impossible to reconcile this [materialist] thought with its antithesis, i.e. dominant bourgeois thought in its sectarian form. The only way to produce such knowledge is to radically and rigorously refute this dominant thought. This refutation starts by drawing a clear epistemological distinction [between dominant bourgeois thought] and materialist thought. Failing to establish such a separation is perhaps the basic mistake made by most adherents of materialist thought who have treated this problem [of sectarianism]. As a result, the question of sectarianism became confused. The premises of materialist thought were conflated with those of its sectarian antithesis, and the process of refuting the latter was thwarted.

Our refutation begins with defining sect and then sectarianism. Either the sect is an independent stand-alone entity, as it is in bourgeois thought, or it is a determined political relation embedded in a particular political system, as it is in materialist thought. In producing knowledge, we must adhere to a self-consistent thought process from start to finish. It is therefore imperative that we define sectarianism in accordance with materialist thought and class analysis: Sectarianism is the particular historical form of the political system through which the Lebanese colonial bourgeoisie exercises its class dominance within a relation of structural dependency on imperialism. Does this mean that 'sectarianism' is particular to this colonial social structure (i.e. dependent capitalism), not to be found in other social structures that preceded it? The answer to this question is a definite yes. But it is only so if we take the concept of 'sectarianism' in this sense as I define here, and not in the widely-held sense – which

 | DOI:10.1163/9789004444249_006

is vague, murky, and imprecisely defined – that it has acquired in its bourgeois conceptualisation. It is quite obvious that 'sectarianism' would be particular to dependent capitalism if this sectarianism were as I define it: the political system of bourgeois domination. For how could this bourgeois political system exist in structures which preceded the existence of the bourgeoisie itself as a dominant class? We have uncritically inherited the concept of 'sectarianism' from bourgeois ideology. This is why I was met with astonishment by those who objected to my assertion that 'sectarianism' must be situated in the structure of colonial relations of production as a bourgeois political system specific and suited to this structure of relations. My [concept of] sectarianism is different from the widely-held meaning these [detractors] had inherited. This is why it is necessary to refute the concept of 'sectarianism' by drawing an epistemological distinction between bourgeois thought and its class negation. With that, I repeat my previous question: Does what I have said mean that the social structures which predated capitalism, such as those of 19th century Lebanon or prior, did not know 'sectarianism'? What about the civil strife of 1860?

I argue that 'sectarianism' – or what is named as such in a language that has come to lack the bare minimum of precision – in those pre-existing structures is something other than what it is in colonial social structures. The material basis of this difference is, specifically, the difference between the former and latter [structures]. It is time for thought, if it truly seeks to produce knowledge, and be therefore materialist thought of a consistent nature, to formulate two different concepts for two different historical realities, or at least to distinguish between two different meanings (or contents) of a single concept (like the concept of 'sectarianism') that differ according to the difference between these two realities signified by that concept.

Section 9: On the History of Sectarianism

There is another question that must be asked: Does what I just said do away with history? Every phenomenon has its history. Does 'sectarianism' not also have a history, one that [Lebanese historian] Massoud Daher and others have attempted to examine? When it comes to this aspect of our subject, the most important task, I argue, is to define both the historical question and the way of posing it, or the form in which it should be posed.

Discourse on the history of sectarianism is meaningless if the sect is not defined in a precise manner. If it were defined in its present reality as the political system in which the Lebanese colonial bourgeoisie exercises its class dominance, then its history would be the history of this very system. In this regard, it is necessary to distinguish between this system's history and the history of its formation, as one is not the same as the other. They do not belong to the same era but, rather, each exists in their own time period. The two are not separated in empirical historical reality by a particular date or event. These histories and eras, moreover, may overlap, and the duration of transition from one to the other may vary depending on specific circumstances. Despite the difficulty of empirically separating between the two, it is imperative to distinguish between them. This distinction is epistemological because it is material. In light of this, perhaps it was the year 1926, when the Lebanese constitution was promulgated during the [French] mandate, that marks the historical beginning of this political system as a sectarian system for bourgeois domination. Perhaps this signpost was the year 1943, when Lebanon became politically independent under the leadership of this bourgeoisie. There is evidence and justification for adopting either of these approaches to identify the beginning of the history of the bourgeois political system as a sectarian system. I will not go into the details of this now. Rather, I want to emphasise the following, namely that if the French Mandate, thanks to the 1926 constitution, laid the (sectarian) foundation of this system, then the Lebanese bourgeoisie subsequently completed this system's construction and strengthened it. It did so over at least the quarter of a century that followed independence – from 1943 to 1967[1] – by establishing institutions for sects that connected the latter to the state in a manner that would guarantee the sects' independence. This means that the sects' institutional existence, which is in effect their existence in a dependent relation to the state, is what guarantees them independence from the state. In this institutional existence and by virtue of it, they appear to be self-sustaining.

In other words, in their very institutional existence, sects are not self-sustaining except through their relation to the state. Their existence as such is the product and historical result of this political system. The history of sectarianism is thus the history of this very system. It is also the history of the class practices – political and ideological – employed by the dominant bourgeoisie with the goal of perpetuating the system of its class dominance. This very history – of this system and these practices – is in its inner movement inseparable from a **counter history**, namely the history of class struggle against this bourgeois class order and these bourgeois class practices. The relation of contradiction between bourgeois history and its counter-history, as it manifests itself in the history of sectarianism, is none other than the relation of contradiction, in the history of class struggle within the Lebanese colonial social

1 Editor's note: Lebanon gained its formal political independence from France in 1943. In 1967, the Supreme Islamic Shia Council was established by a parliamentary decree as the official religious body representing the Shia sect in emulation of other similar bodies like the Maronite Church and Dar al-Fatwa (representing the Sunni sect).

structure, between the following: the ruling bourgeoisie on one hand – with its sectarian system (which is the system of its class dominance) and its sectarian practices (which are its class practices) – and the toiling classes on the other hand (the working class and its allies) with its class practices, whether in opposition or in submission to that system.

The history of sectarianism is therefore the history of the transformation of this relation of class contradiction. It is not strange, therefore, that our examination of the history of sectarianism as a history of a bourgeois political system and of bourgeois class practices leads us to examine the history of the class struggle against the bourgeoisie as a history of struggle against this [sectarian] system and these practices. In fact, it is necessary – [rather than strange] – that this history of sectarianism is simultaneously a history and counter-history. This is so because this history of sectarianism is itself the history of the class struggle, and of the forms taken by this struggle and its instruments in the Lebanese colonial social structure. The movement of contradiction in this history is therefore between the bourgeoisie and the working class, or we could say the dominant and toiling classes in this structure. It is a *contradictory* history. This is because this history is viewed differently from the standpoint of the dominant bourgeoisie compared to the standpoint of the working classes. In the former's view, it might be as I said a history of a system and of institutions, and maybe a history of sects as well. Because it is such, it is a history that recedes into what preceded the colonial structure. It is an extension of what came before by which the present is identified with the past without distinction, i.e. in a manner which necessarily conceals the perpetuation of the existing bourgeois system. This is the concealment of both the relation of class dominance specific to the colonial bourgeoisie and of the system of its rule, whose renewal is conditional on the structural relation of dependency to imperialism (the colonial relation). In the second case, i.e. when this history is viewed from the standpoint of the working class, it is necessarily a history of class struggle against this system and its institutions, i.e. against sects and the bourgeois system of these sects' institutional existence, a system that is one and the same as the political system for bourgeois rule. This, precisely, is the history of sectarianism, which has no other history, except for what resides as illusions in dominant bourgeois ideology.

As for the history of the formation of sectarianism, it is the history of the formation of the bourgeois political system, which is inseparable from the history of the formation of the Lebanese social structure as a colonial structure. This system arose and was constituted as a sectarian order within this structure and its own formation. The movement of this formation is complex. It is the [twin] movement of the dismantling of the previous social structure – let us call it the feudal structure – and the building-up of the new capitalist structure. These two connected movements comprise a single, complex movement in which each of the two defines and is defined by the other. The dismantling of the feudal structure is conditional on the formation of new capitalist relations, a process that is [in turn] conditional on the dismantling of the previous structure. The sectarian question brings us back to the conditions of this single, complex historical movement of the dismantling of the old and formation of the new. This question is as follows: What are the specific historical conditions in which the Lebanese bourgeois political order formed as a sectarian order?

Perhaps it is wise to pose another, broader question. First, namely, why did the Lebanese bourgeois political system turn out to be sectarian? This question straddles the structural and the historical, so to speak. Its answer is as follows: This order came out as a sectarian order because it formed under specific historical conditions that explain its specific formation. The historical question at hand thus takes the following form: Which conditions explain the bourgeois system in its sectarian form? The basis of such an explanation, in the final analysis, is that capitalism in Lebanon entered its crisis phase as it entered its formation phase. Capitalism began to form in Lebanon during the crisis phase of the capitalist mode of production, namely its phase of transition to imperialism. Thus we find that the crisis of the development of imperialism, which is the crisis of capitalist development, lies at the basis of the formation of the bourgeois political order as a sectarian order. The organic link between sectarianism and imperialism appears, therefore, in the formation of the Lebanese social structure as a colonial structure. The history of the formation of sectarianism, as outlined above, traces its beginnings to the mid-nineteenth century. By that I am not saying that this history began with some specific event or set of events, such as those of 1860. What I mean, rather, is that it is traceable to a structure in-formation, specifically to the beginning of the formation of capitalist relations of production under the aegis of capitalist imperialist penetration, the disintegration of feudal relations – in a relative, distinct historical form – and the breakup of the Ottoman state. Tracing this history to what existed before these relations of production, without distinguishing between the different social eras before and after their formation, leads to nothing but ambiguity when treating the sectarian question, especially its historical dimension.

Chapter 7: The Political System: Between Sectarian Reform and the Necessity of Democratic Change[2]

Part Two: On Sectarian Balance

Section 1: On Hegemonic Balance

Sectarian balance, which is necessary for the existence of the [Lebanese] state and its longevity as a sectarian state does not mean equality between the sects, even if this balance's ideological function is to inspire such equality or produce an illusion of equality in our minds. On the contrary, it is a hegemonic balance that is established only by a sectarian balance [i.e. hegemony of a single sect], which ensures the existence of this balance as sectarian. The real problem here is not in this hegemony's existence, or lack thereof, but in the relation between class hegemony and sectarian hegemony established within the state. The Lebanese state exists in a deadlocked contradiction that defines its structure, whereby this contradiction is that between Lebanon as a bourgeois state, on the one hand, and Lebanon as a sectarian state, on the other. It is in light of this structural contradiction that we can understand the hegemonic balance at hand. The position of class hegemony, which is foundational to the state's existence as a bourgeois state, necessarily has a sectarian character in the Lebanese state due to the latter's sectarian character. Class hegemony in this state thus necessarily appears as sectarian hegemony, which in turn is the condition for the state to perform its class function as a bourgeois state. For further analysis of this topic, the reader may consult the eighth paragraph of the third chapter of my book, *An Introduction to the Refutation of Sectarian Thought*.[3]

Since we have carried out this analysis elsewhere, we do not desire to repeat it here. Recent events have unfolded quickly. They have sped up the disintegration of the system of rule of the *Kataeb* party.[4] The latter had sought fascism to salvage the sectarian order of rotten bourgeois dominance, thereby aiding its collapse. With these recent events in mind, and with seeking to identify the form that radical and now much-needed political change could take, we present the following idea for discussion:

The hegemonic nature of the sectarian balance is what guarantees the possibility for the state to perform its class function as a bourgeois state. This

2 This was originally published in [the Lebanese Communist Party's] newspaper *al-Nidaa* as a series of successive articles starting on 4 March 1984.

3 Editor's note: See Amel 1980.

4 Editor's note: The Kataeb, or Phalanges, was the main right-wing Lebanese political party that colluded with Israel during the civil war and whose leader Amin Gemayel was President of Lebanon at the time when Amel wrote this book.

balance was foundational to the state's existence for various historical reasons, the details of which we cannot discuss here. However, the civil war – in its many phases as well as in the democratic struggles that preceded it – has affirmed in concrete historical terms that the sectarian balance no longer guarantees this possibility for the state. Rather, it stands as the foremost obstacle preventing the state from performing this function [as a bourgeois state]. The movement of class struggles burst open, through violence, the deadlocked contradiction latent in the structure of the Lebanese state. This movement necessitated an alteration in this balance and in the state's sectarian form [if the sectarian system were to survive]. The question confronting us here is whether 'participation' [via power sharing] is to bring about this [needed] change [for the survival of the sectarian system]. Does participation present a solution? Does it resolve the state's deadlocked contradiction? 'Participation' is a concept that has been discussed at length, but imprecisely, even as it has been raised as a slogan for a potential solution. But is it truly the solution?

Section 2: On the Concept of 'Participation'

In preparing to answer this question, we can say that the concept of 'participation' contains a diagnosis of the problem: it assumes that the problem is the existence of sectarian hegemony over the state (as though the state occupies a neutral or external position in relation to the 'sects', classes, and their struggles, as though the state is sought as an entity independent of them). In this scheme, ending sectarian hegemony is accomplished via participating in it [by the marginalised sects]. [According to this logic], rather than one sect, namely the Maronites, monopolising power, the latter should be exercised as agreed-upon in the arrangement of 1943: participation between two sects, namely the Maronites and the Sunnis (see Michel Chiha).[5] The problem, accordingly, is that one of the two parties, [namely the Maronites], breached the sectarian contract and appropriated what belonged to both. Other parties [i.e. other sects] then came forward to demand what these two [sects] had. As more players entered the game, the contract fell apart. The Maronites and Sunnis held executive power by which – without legislative power? – they achieved hegemony. The seat of executive power is also the seat of hegemony. The latter only goes to whoever has the former. The solution, then, would be reform that rectifies the state by way of participatory sectarian rule (between two, three,

5 Editor's note: Michel Chiha was the foremost ideologue of Lebanese nationalism in the first half of the twentieth century and one of the architects of the Lebanese constitution of 1926 and the national pact of 1943.

six, or even more parties?), thus regaining the cohesion that the state lost in its original conceptualisation as a sectarian state.

Bluntly speaking, this solution is born out of nostalgia on the part of certain sections of the dominant bourgeoisie for a bygone era before a crisis hit the system. In that period, these (Islamic) sections shared power, via their sectarian representatives, in the near-total political absence of [their sect's] toiling classes. These [sections] accepted scraps of power in return for submitting to and accepting a hegemony [of their Maronite counterparts] that they [eventually] came to refuse, or, more precisely, whose severity they sought to reduce so as to preserve their position in this system and thus also to preserve the system itself. This was especially true after the toiling classes began to take shape as an independent political force and to liberate themselves from their previous form of existence as sects in a long, complex process of becoming through democratic national resistance movements. The solution of 'participation' presented by these sectors similarly expresses their ambitions to strengthen their positions of power, i.e. to change their positions within the sectarian political system – but not to change the system itself – so as to re-distribute hegemony and its positions of power. In sum, the reform that certain sections of the bourgeoisie assumed to be possible via participation – if this participation were to come to be, or if achieving it were possible – would ultimately entrench and reinforce the sectarian political system rather than change and eliminate it. Their solution is thus not a solution after all. It is, rather, a deepening of the system's crisis.

For clarity's sake, it must be stated that the concept of 'participation' falls within the belief system of bourgeois ideology in its determination as a sectarian ideology. This concept's identification with the bourgeois class appears, specifically, in its erasure of the class character of the system of sectarian balance, as well as in its framing of problems and their solutions as involving sects alone, with total disregard to classes and class conflict. To simply state this is insufficient as a critique of the concept of 'participation', and there are more important facets to this critique than what we have covered. 'Participation', in some aspect, may be a utopian solution to an actual crisis, i.e. an illusory solution to the real crisis at hand. This illusory solution lies in eliminating disadvantages of the sectarian system without eliminating the system itself, i.e. eliminating hegemony in the system by dividing it between more than one sect.

Section 3: An Illusory Solution

The illusory nature, class character, and ideological significance of the 'participatory' solution [whereby side-lined sects partake in power] renders it similar to the solution proposed by populism – that petit-bourgeois trend – for the crisis of capitalism. This latter solution calls for the elimination of the disadvantages of the capitalist system without actually eliminating it, i.e. by an illusory elimination of its structural contradictions and its pernicious effects. Such a shift in [class] consciousness towards a form of class illusion characterises the consciousness of the non-hegemonic bourgeois factions in its (legitimate?) ambition to occupy the position of the hegemonic faction of the dominant bourgeoisie, whether by replacing the existing one or through sharing its position, and to emulate it politically and economically, if possible. The utopian slogans that these bourgeois factions rally behind in particular circumstances are nothing more than an expression of these ambitions and their inability to achieve them. Examples of such slogans include 'justice' or 'equality', meaning justice and equality among factions of the dominant bourgeoisie, so that no faction of this class has hegemony over another.

Like the idea of dissolving class differences, 'participation' is but another of these utopian slogans, governed by the same logic of class illusion specific to the consciousness of non-hegemonic factions of the dominant bourgeoisie. According to this logic, the hegemony of the dominant class's hegemonic faction must be eliminated while maintaining that class's dominance. In the case of 'participation', this is the logic of eliminating sectarian hegemony without eliminating the dominance of sects, in other words, without eliminating the system of their dominance. This system of sectarian dominance is one and the same as the system of the dominant bourgeoisie's class dominance. This logic is utopian, i.e. the logic of class illusion, because the bourgeoisie cannot attain class dominance except through the presence of a hegemonic faction. This faction's class hegemony is thus foundational to the dominance of all factions of the dominant class without distinction, and it guarantees the everlasting renewal of this class dominance. The elimination of this hegemony and its system leads – by necessity of its logic – to the elimination of this [entire] class dominance, i.e. its system [of dominance]. Such an elimination occurs through a complex trajectory of class conflict, which unfolds in different forms and phases subject to historical circumstances.

Section 4: Disabling the Role of the State

In light of the above, we repeat that a sectarian balance occurs only through hegemony, not participation. A sectarian state cannot arise except under such a hegemonic balance. This is not born out of [some] sectarian necessity (or some divine wisdom that confers hegemony on a particular sect, namely the Maronite sect. [Such wisdom is conferred] because the sect is what it is according to the sectarian racism of the fascist approach that – in this ongoing civil war, and until further notice – the hegemonic faction of the dominant bourgeoisie has chosen as its approach to class struggle against nationalist and democratic forces, and as a result against non-hegemonic factions of the bourgeoisie itself). Rather, this hegemonic balance is born out of class necessity, namely the necessity of the state in its class existence as a state. This is because power, since it is state power, necessarily has a hegemonic character. Power does not exist except in this form of state power that is one and the same as hegemony. Hegemony belongs to whoever is in power. Every elimination of hegemony is thus necessarily the elimination of power, i.e. of the power of the state, specifically. How can a state assume its class function when the position of hegemony within the state has been eliminated and, as a result, its power? This is what compels us to say without reservation that sectarian 'participation', with its connotation or goal of eliminating sectarian hegemony within the framework of the sectarian state while also preserving that state, is impossible by definition within a centralised state, even if some try to achieve it in practice. If participation were to be achieved, it would ultimately disable the state and nullify its class function by eliminating the position of hegemony, which is the seat of power in a centralised state. 'Participation' thus either paralyses a centralised state or multiplies the positions of hegemony and power within it and – according to the state's sectarian logic – effectually multiplies the state. The centralised state thus shatters into multiple sectarian statelets governed by the principle of political decentralisation.

The logic of the existence of the bourgeois state as a sectarian state – the very logic of the state's deadlocked contradiction – is what underlies the possibility of its multiplication into sectarian mini-states. With this multiplication, the state's theoretical conceptualisation as a sectarian state is actualised through the disappearance of its existence as a bourgeois state. This is how the bourgeois state disintegrates. The logic of its sectarian existence – the basis of its bourgeois existence – is brought to its ultimate conclusion. It is as though, in its inability to exist as a bourgeois state, and with its culmination in a state of sects, the state fulfils its theoretical conceptualisation as a bourgeois colonial state that is impotent by definition. As the present civil war rages on, history is confirming this logic [of impotence] by displaying the inability of the Lebanese bourgeoisie and its sectarian system to unify society, people, and nation. Given that sectarian-based reform according to the 'participation' principle is anything but, we ask: Could another kind of sectarian-based reform be possible? And if so what would it be and under what conditions?

(A side note: Like the similar if not identical principle of 'participation', the principle of equitable power sharing between sects is impossible to implement if the state is to remain a state given that the latter is only possible under the condition of hegemony. The actual implementation of the principle of equitable power sharing, despite the theoretical impossibility of this happening – would necessarily culminate in the crippling and paralysis of the state).

Section 5: Substituting One Hegemony for Another

Could the desired sectarian-based solution be replacing the existing sectarian hegemony with another sectarian hegemony – such as Shia or Druze hegemony or otherwise?

Such a solution is no solution at all. The fault does not lie with one sect, as though a particular sect is the disease that must be eradicated. This idea reflects sectarian racism akin to that at the core of Zionism or the fascist sectarianism of the Kataeb [party]. The fault lies, rather, in the political system's existence as a sectarian system, and in the state's existence as a sectarian state. As we have shown, the sect is not a real entity, but a political relation that is renewed and perpetuated as the sectarian system is renewed and perpetuated. This system is what maintains this relation and guarantees its reproduction. The system's existence in turn guarantees the perpetual renewal of class dominance by the dominant bourgeoisie as well as the hegemony of its hegemonic faction, namely the financial oligarchy. It clearly follows that the collective existence of all sects – not the existence of a single one – is contingent upon the existence of the sectarian system, which is nothing but the system of bourgeois class dominance based on the hegemony of the financial oligarchy. The end of this system spells the end of sects (in the political sense already specified, not in the sense of religious affiliation illustrated in, for example, sectarian devotional practices), since sects do not exist except by and in this system, insofar as it is the system in which they exist in relations of hegemonic balance. This means that it is the system as a whole, as a unity of relations of its constituents, that exists as opposed to the existence of its separate parts.

Section 6: On the *Kataeb* Project

We should read the Kataeb project and its failure in light of the previous analysis. Its sectarian character is not determined by its affiliation with a particular sect, namely the Maronite sect (despite the Kataeb's Maronite character and real ambitions to turn a racially pure Maronite sect into the backbone of its dreamt-up Christian nationalist state). Rather, this sectarian character is determined by the Kataeb's affiliation with the sectarian system, insofar as it is the system of bourgeois domination. In other words, this project is determined, due to its very class character, by its affiliation with this dominant bourgeoisie. In political practice, the Kataeb project thus embodies the attempt by the bourgeoisie, particularly its financial oligarchy, to salvage the bourgeoisie's sectarian system by seeking a fascist solution to this system's intractable crisis. The project was an attempt to remove the physical obstacles – which had begun to increase with shocking speed – to the mechanism by which bourgeois class dominance was renewed. The Kataeb and its sectarian fascist project had direct, systematic, and multi-faceted support from, first, the state and all bourgeois factions regardless of sect (including the Islamic factions), and second, the reactionary Arab regimes that funded the project.

It is beyond the scope of this brief article to analyse these obstacles, which I have treated in detail elsewhere (namely in my book *Inquiry into the Causes of the Civil War in Lebanon*).[6] It is enough to say here that foremost among these obstacles was the mass of toilers who belong to the downtrodden 'sects' and live either in the countryside or in the clutches of poverty in the capital. As their voices were raised, so did their acts of resistance. They demanded the system be changed, whether by putting an end to sectarian hegemony without destroying the system itself, or by putting an end to the system entirely. In sum, the conditions which determined the system of bourgeois dominance as a sectarian system also determined the sectarian, racist character of the fascist solution to this system's crisis. This system's transition from sectarian democracy (i.e. the hegemonic balance which relies on the political destruction of the sectarian antithesis to the bourgeoisie) to sectarian fascism confirms the depth of the crisis and dilemma of the bourgeoisie in generating a solution to it. This sectarian fascism – especially as utilised by the 'Lebanese Forces' and Kataeb party as an instrument of the bourgeoisie and in service of its system – means, in practice before theory, substituting sectarian coexistence with sectarian singularity and purifying inter-sectarian mixing, which must be eradicated to achieve sectarian racial purity.

Section 7: On the Failure of the Fascist Solution

This solution is doomed to fail. It may be the ideal solution to reform this sectarian system from within. It presumably endows each sect with its own canton-like statelet in which sectarian purity is preserved. Yet in reality it eliminates sects politically – except for one that alone possesses the right to exist as a sect because it alone is eligible for this existence – while striving for their material elimination. For it aspires, in a utopian fashion, to build a Christian (indeed a Maronite) nationalist state along the lines of the Jewish state. It seeks to emulate the Jewish state in a caricaturist fashion while allying itself with that state in a racist and dependent manner. This [Maronite] state would be a haven for Christians of the East and the 'free' World's bridgehead into the heart of the

6 Editor's note: See Amel 1979.

Arab World. This 'ideal' sectarian-based reform, as we have already suggested, eliminates the state as a bourgeois state, or at least impedes its class function. If this solution came to pass, the state would collapse upon itself and break into pieces. Such is the dilemma of the bourgeoisie and its sectarian system, and with every solution it attempts, the hole in which it finds itself gets deeper.

The fact that the fascist solution is logically doomed to fail is not enough for it to fail. It had to be scuttled. The struggles of the national democratic forces over the years of the ongoing civil war did so in tangible political terms. History always runs according to a logic and as a materialist movement of class struggles by which different possible histories are generated. In this movement, necessity in history is actualised through diverse ideological forms of consciousness that do not necessarily align with the logic ruling it or with the objective realities that conflicting social forces occupy in the field of the class struggle.

Section 8: On Sectarian Projects

In this context, we want to suggest that scuttling the Kataeb project, which embodies the fascist sectarian solution to the crisis of the sectarian system of the Lebanese bourgeoisie's domination, is simultaneously a defeat of all other possible sectarian projects. It equally undercuts the expectations harboured by some forces for projects of this kind, whether they aim to substitute one sectarian hegemony for another or to establish some form of an equitable sectarian power-sharing arrangement. All such projects rest on a single foundation, namely the existence of the political system as a sectarian system, and the consolidation of the state as a sectarian state. There are no possible sectarian alternatives to the Kataeb sectarian project, as all such 'alternatives' in fact fall under this project's banner. The various projects with sectarian solutions to the crisis of the sectarian system become incoherent once the fascist solution, which has undercut the viability of these projects, becomes incoherent. The fascist solution was a radical attempt to reform the sectarian bourgeois system from within. It bore the very logic at the root of this system, namely that of a deadlocked contradiction. Thus every other sectarian reform was subordinate and less radical. As the fascist solution reached a dead end, so did every other sectarian-based avenue for reform. The entire system closed onto its sectarian self. It became necessary to change this system in order to allow any historical development of Lebanon to take place. The only avenue of change is national democratic [change], which is the antithesis of the fascist solution. Do all of the social forces that joined the battle to scuttle this fascist solution realise that they themselves are the forces of this national democratic change?

Section 9: A Contradiction That Must Be Resolved

We pose this question with the intent of pointing out that some forces partook and continue to partake in this battle – [while armed with] ideological forms of consciousness that are sectarian. Perhaps their ambitions are limited to rectifying this system of sectarian rule so as to effect an exchange in the positions of hegemony in this system between sects for the benefit of some and at the expense of others, possibly on the basis of each sect's percentage of the population, or on some other basis. It is not important to delve into the details of the shapes sectarian reform could take in the dreams and aspirations of one or another party among the forces resisting fascist sectarian hegemony. Rather, it is important to remember – when inquiring into and discussing the matter at hand – that it is necessary to distinguish between the objective course of history's movement and the ideological forms of consciousness through which this course is actualised. We must, therefore, distinguish between the actual position that these forces occupy in the field of the class struggle through their resistance to fascist sectarian hegemony, and between the ideological form of consciousness in which they fight against this hegemony and which is, for some of them, sectarian. Naturally, the democratic character of these forces' resistance is not determined by the sectarian form of their social consciousness. Rather, it is determined by the actual position that they occupy in the field of class struggle, insofar as it is the position of opposition to fascism and sectarian hegemony. This position exists in this field in an antagonistic relation of struggle to the opposing fascist position, a class position, even if it takes a sectarian form on the level of consciousness.

An actual contradiction thus exists between these forces' position in the field of the class struggle against fascism and its sectarian hegemony, which is necessarily the revolutionary class position, and between the sectarian form of consciousness with which they perceive their relation to this position, as well as their relation to their political practices and even to the historical horizon of its own struggle. Naturally, it is possible that this contradiction becomes an obstacle in the development of the revolution's course. What we want to emphasise in this regard, however, is the following: [firstly], these forces' fight against the hegemony of sectarian fascism is the main challenge to the sectarian reform that these same forces could be aspiring to achieve. [Secondly], the success of this fight is that system's demise. It is as though these forces bear the logic of history, which pushes them to make up their mind once and for all. Either they go against the reactionary sectarian form of their ideological consciousness, i.e. in the direction of radically changing the sectarian political system of rule by the dominant bourgeoisie, or they align with this same reactionary sectarian consciousness – (but against the class interests of their toiling factions) – and lean towards sectarian reform of this system. In the latter case, the system would catch its breath in a movement that would renew its crisis, and subsequently the conditions for civil war.

Conclusion: Novelty in This Phase

In sum: the logic of opposition to the hegemony of sectarian fascism is one and the same as the logic that opens up the horizon of national democratic change in history. We can say, with total clarity, that the termination of the system of this hegemony is not only the termination of all other projects built on sectarian solutions, but also, in the first degree, the termination of the very system of the financial oligarchy's hegemony. This, precisely, is what is new in our current historical phase. Also new is the fact that Lebanon, having been led by the bourgeoisie (itself led by the financial oligarchy) to destruction, will not rise again except on the wreckage of its sectarian political system. It will do so united against that system and this bourgeoisie, in national resistance against Israeli occupation and imperialist invasion. The bourgeoisie failed in building and uniting the country. Thanks to its system [of rule], the bourgeoisie founded a country already broken and led it to fragmentation. To save itself, it surrendered the country to an Israeli occupation. It sought the latter, backed by imperialist fleets, to subdue what it surrendered. It was thus upon us, we the multitude of toilers, to liberate the country with a resistance that builds it anew in freedom and for freedom, as a country for the people and not for sects. In a time of revolutionary change, the future is ours.

CHAPTER 6

Marx in the Orientalism of Edward Said

Book Title:
Does the Heart Belong to the East and the Mind to the West? Marx in the Orientalism of Edward Said
Beirut: Dar al-Farabi, 3rd edition, 2006. (First published in 1985).

In a four-page segment of *Orientalism*,[1] a work that continues to be discussed with great interest in the Arab World and beyond, Edward Said considers Marx's relationship with the Orient and Orientalist thought. It is a passage worth pausing to reflect upon. My aim in this article is to discuss this single excerpt, limited to pages 170 to 173 out of the 366-page Arabic edition.[2]

1 Thought of the Nation or the Dominant Class?

In the Saidian text, we read the following, '… what the early Orientalist achieved, and what the non-Orientalist in the West exploited, was a reduced model of the Orient suitable for the prevailing, dominant culture and its theoretical (and hard after the theoretical, the practical) exigencies'.[3]

I begin with this passage to introduce the reader to the framework of the basic argument which guides Said's thought throughout his book. The Orient discussed by Orientalism is not the actual Orient, but an 'Orient' that is produced by Orientalist thought in its own image, and as such is 'suitable for the prevailing, dominant culture'. In the West, this is the culture of the dominant bourgeoisie. Rather than explicitly specify this culture's historical class character, the Saidian text describes it as Western-European culture. It is 'prevailing' and 'dominant' [according to Said] because it is Western culture rather than the fact that it is the culture of the dominant bourgeoisie. In disavowing this culture's historical class character, Said's definition disavows the possibility that there may exist an antithesis to it. This culture thereby acquires [in Said's definition] a universal character that suggests it constitutes all that is [denoted by

1 Said 1981.
2 Said 2003, pp. 153–7 in the English edition.
3 Said 1981, pp. 153, 170 in the Arabic edition.

 | DOI:10.1163/9789004444249_007

the word] culture. This is precisely what this particular culture strives for from its position of dominance. Indeed, it aspires to nullify all that is other than itself, and to make itself appear as culture per se. There is, however, a difference between its real historical existence as dominant bourgeois culture (i.e. the culture of the dominant class) and the form that it endeavours to take as 'culture' writ large, or as the culture of the nation (*umma*) as a whole. In the process of struggle and contradiction between dominant class thought and its antithesis, viewing history from the position of dominant class thought, even if through a critical lens, eliminates this difference. Viewing history from the point of view of thought opposed to dominant thought, asserts this difference.

This is why it is necessary for historical thought to be materialist in order for it to be scientific. Thought that equates the external form of something with the thing itself, on the other hand, elides the contradiction and conflict between ideas in the history of thought. In so doing, it accepts a unitary [conception] of culture because it sees culture itself in 'prevailing, dominant thought' and thereby leaves no potential for its antithesis to exist. At the very least we should call this thought idealist for viewing history from the vantage point of dominant thought, even if it attempts to oppose this thought.

As I see it, this kind of thinking governs Said's perception of Marx and Marx's relationship with Orientalist thought. Directly after the previously quoted passage, Said writes:

> Occasionally one comes across exceptions, or if not exceptions then interesting complications, to this unequal partnership between East and West. Karl Marx identified the notion of an Asiatic economic system in his 1853 analyses of British rule in India, and then put beside that immediately the human depredation introduced into this system by English colonial interference, rapacity, and outright cruelty. In article after article he returned with increasing conviction to the idea that even in destroying Asia, Britain was making possible there a real social revolution. Marx's style pushes us right up against the difficulty of reconciling our natural repugnance as fellow creatures to the sufferings of Orientals while their society is being violently transformed with the historical necessity of these transformations.[4]

Let us take a moment to examine this passage before turning to the text by Marx that Said discusses.

---

4 Said 2003, p. 153; Said 1981, p. 170.

Said's argument runs as follows: there is an unequal partnership between East and West constructed by Orientalist thought. No Western scholar – even if he is not an Orientalist – escapes this. What this means is that all Western thought sees the Orient through the lens of orientalism. This 'Orient' is not the Orient itself, but the Orient that Orientalism has constructed. It follows that the relationship between the West and the Orient is governed by the logic of Orientalist thought and there is no escaping it for any [Western] thought, not even Marx's. The previously cited excerpt from *Orientalism* clearly affirms this *general principle*, which – according to Said – holds true for Marx as it does for others. The problem is not, therefore, a problem of this or that individual thinker. At its core, it is a matter of principle. The dominant thought in a given nation is this nation's thought that governs the thinking of all its individuals. This is true for Orientalist thought, according to which all Western scholars think, as 'No scholar ... can resist the pressures on him of his nation or of the scholarly tradition in which he works'.[5]

This is the general law of thought formulated by Edward Said. It rests on the erasure of the historical class character of ideas, and thus also on the erasure of the movement of struggle and contradiction between them. As he portrays it, the intellectual field is that of dominant thought alone, and the structure of this field is simple. This is because it is confined to the structure of the [supposedly] only thought there is, i.e. dominant thought. The structure of this field does not therefore reflect its material, socio-historical reality, which is a complex structure of many contradictory, conflicting intellectual structures that exist in a historical movement unified by the struggles between social classes. In Said's formulation, by contrast, it is a monolithic structure – namely that of the dominant class – synonymous with the entire nation's thought. By such a proposition – in which the reader can discern some features of what, in our political parlance, is called 'nationalist thought' – the internal relation of contradiction in the ideological struggle between conflicting intellectual structures is turned into an external relation of contradiction between the thought of the nation and the thought of the individual. The individual is incapable of using his own thinking to resist his nation's dominant thought. This dominant thought always prevails in the end because it imposes itself upon the individual, as mandated by the general law that governs the history of thought [as Said sees it]. According to this law, no individual can escape the dominance of nationalist thought except 'occasionally', which is to say, in *exceptional* cases. If such a case does in fact exist, it proves rather than undermines nationalist

5 Said 2003, p. 271; Said 1981, p. 273.

thought. Indeed, the exception proves the rule insofar as it is an aberration. In the field of thought, this exception is actually the antithesis of dominant, prevailing thought. The following question might present itself: Why should dominant thought of the dominant class be deemed, as the rule, while its antithesis rendered as the exception? The answer lies in the very law or general principle that the author of *Orientalism* presents for thought in general. Indeed, the logic governing Said's thinking is none other than the logic of identification.

…

3 Does the Heart Belong to the East and the Mind to the West?

It is helpful for the reader to understand which of Marx's ideas are defined [by Said] as the exception to the [Orientalist] rule, and which of them count [as Orientalist]. Returning to the Saidian text, we find that Marx [is said to] depart from Orientalist thinking with his denunciation of Easterners' suffering [under British imperialism]. He is then said to submissively fall back in line with Orientalist thought in his statement about the historical necessity of the transformations underway in Eastern societies. This interpretation should give us pause not only because it is a misunderstanding of Marx, but also for what it reveals about the structure of thought underlying Edward Said's interpretation of these Marxian texts.

According to Said, Marx breaks away from the structure of Orientalist thought when he speaks of feelings, emotion, and sensitivity, in short when he speaks from the heart. As soon as Marx, however, applies reason, he reverts back into an Orientalist mode of thinking. It is as though Marx [as interpreted by Said] is caught in a battle between the mind and the heart, with his heart belonging to the East and his mind to the West. If the heart speaks and the mind is silent, Orientalist thought is overcome. But as soon as reason is evoked, [Orientalist] thought is reaffirmed via the affirmation of historical necessity by Marxist thought. A seemingly unresolvable contradiction emerges between what Edward Said calls 'human sympathy'[6] and objective, scientific analysis of historical necessity. They are mutually exclusive. If thought affirms the former, it stands in defence of the East against Orientalism, and if it affirms the latter, it affirms by extension Orientalism, i.e. it adopts a Western standpoint opposed to the East. It is as though every scientific or rational approach to the Orient necessarily falls into the logic of Orientalism, which is to say the logic of Western

6 Said 2003, p. 163; no page number is given for the Arabic edition.

thought. It is as though this thought is rational insofar as it is Western thought. Meanwhile, the only approach to [understanding] the East capable of delivering the thinker from the danger of falling in the logic of Western thought is a heartfelt *spiritual*, as opposed to rational, approach, i.e. an approach from the standpoint of 'identifying' with 'the vital forces' informing 'Eastern culture', and from a position of 'identification' with it. According to Said, herein lies 'Massignon's greatest contribution' to the field of Oriental studies, with [the French Orientalist's] approach to the Orient based on 'individual intuition of spiritual dimensions'.[7] This is what sets Massignon apart from all other Orientalists; his spirit identified with the spirit of the East. This approach [according to Said] enabled Massignon to overcome the structure of Orientalist thought, or to occasionally transgress the boundaries of its structure. We say 'occasionally' here so as not to put words in the author's mouth and accuse him of saying something that he did not. Despite his intense admiration for Massignon's spiritual ability to identify with the 'vital forces' of the East in his scholarship, Said sees that 'in one direction [Massignon's] ideas about the Orient remained thoroughly traditional and Orientalist, their personality and remarkable eccentricity notwithstanding'. Yet Said does not specify, at least in this text, which direction of Massignon's thinking he is referring to. To prove this, we will reproduce the relevant passage in its entirety, even though we have already quoted some parts:

> No scholar, not even Massignon, can resist the pressures on him of his nation or of the scholarly tradition in which he works. In a great deal of what he said of the Orient and its relationship with the Occident, Massignon seemed to refine and yet to repeat the ideas of other French Orientalists. We must allow, however, that the refinements, the personal style, the individual genius, may finally supersede the political restrains operating impersonally through tradition and through the national ambience. Even so, in Massignon's case we must also recognise that in one direction his ideas about the Orient remained thoroughly traditional and Orientalist, their personality and remarkable eccentricity notwithstanding.[8]

As we have seen, the text begins by laying out a general principle for nationalist thought that [it claims] is as true for Massignon as it is for Marx. We are citing these two names together because they are the only two possible exceptions

7 Said 2003, p. 265; Said 1981, p. 268.

8 Said 2003, p. 271; Said 1981, p. 273 (as cited by Amel).

alluded to in *Orientalism*, and because each is given as an example that sheds light on the other. They also shed light on *Orientalism*'s method of analysis and the general logic of its author's thinking. The critique of this logic is what constitutes the critique of the Saidian critical interpretation or reading of the Marxian text. *Orientalism* insists that no one, not even Massignon or Marx, is excluded from this principle of nationalist thought. The text, however, qualifies its earlier claim and opens the window of possibility for an exception. It does so in suggesting, on an abstract level of thought, the possibility that individual genius may be capable of violating the principle that governs the thought of the nation as a whole. But this possibility is not necessarily existent; rather, it is arbitrary or accidental. In other words, the existence of such genius is beyond the scope of reason and rational principles, since individual genius is only defined in contradistinction to the thought of the nation, which is one and the same as thought writ large. It is as if *Orientalism*'s author is implicitly invoking in this vein a common premise of prevalent, i.e. dominant thought in the nineteenth century. That premise substituted class-based *contradiction* at the heart of the social relationship, whether in the field of thought, politics or economics, with another contradiction that is *individual in nature*, which is to say that it exists between the individual and society, i.e. between the individual and the nation or state.

The individual-nation contradiction is only possible according to the [logic] of nationalist thought. Within the limits of this field of nationalist thought, the movement of this contradiction can take no path other than that determined by one component of the contradiction, the nation, to the exclusion of the other component, the individual. Nationalist thought thereby is always in a dominant position within such a contradiction. The thought of the nation thus maintains constant dominance in this contradiction, thanks to the very nature of this contradiction. The unfolding of this contradiction is what perpetuates this dominance. Even when individual thought breaks away from it. In a contradiction between individual and nation – whether in the realm of thought or not – the individual is always going to be crushed into [sic] the nation, even if he is an anomaly. As for the nation, it is eternal as though it were an ever-renewable or essentially permanent absolute. History, in the movement of this contradiction, is nothing more than the history of a nation constantly asserting itself against individual opposition. Viewed through this lens, history does not appear to be history given that the West is the West – one and the same since ancient Greece until the present. Alternatively, history appears as though it is the antithesis of history in the sense that nationalist thought, for instance, does not allow for or tolerate novelty. This is because all new thought comes from the individual, but the individual is incapable – even if he has the genius of Massignon or Marx – to 'resist the pressures of his nation' (these pressures being at once intellectual, political, and non-political) or to break away from the structure of this nation's dominant thought. Indeed, the individual cannot escape this structure of thought at work in his national context. According to this theory of nationalist thought (the sources of which we will discern later), all change falls within an existing intellectual structure and works to preserve it. Change is not actually change, therefore, but the form in which this intellectual structure is forever renewed and maintained. Change from without is thus necessarily individual in character dominant thought of the nation, which is national in character. Individual thought is incapable of changing national thought, even if it breaks away from it.

In discussing Massignon and Marx as two exceptional cases in the history of Orientalist thought, Edward Said attempts to prove this theory of nationalist thought. While both thinkers oppose their nation's thought in their hearts, they return to it in their minds. Massignon is spiritually united with the East through his spiritual approach to it, which enables him to escape from the traditional structure of Orientalist thought. Yet in one line of thinking about the East [as Said informs us in the following quote,] Massignon falls back into this structure: 'Massignon's implication is that the essence of the difference between East and West is between modernity and ancient tradition. (Author's note: We did not find this sentence in the French text). And indeed in his writings on political and contemporary problems, which is where one can see most immediately the limitations of Massignon's method, the East-West opposition turns up in a most peculiar way'.[9]

In this text, Said clearly determines the realm in which Massignon's thought remains traditional and Orientalist – namely in his treatment of modernity and, specifically, of [modern] politics. In this manner, Said affirms the impossibility of an individual opposing national thought and of resisting its political pressures. This excerpt, we should note, also contains another, more dangerous, idea, namely that [Massignon's] ideas about modernity and those about the [pre-modern Eastern] heritage are different. If those of the former were orientalist, those of the latter offer a valid representation of their subject. The spiritual approach is thereby affirmed as solely capable of converging with its subject. Is there not something of an affirmation in this statement of the traditional Orientalist idea which distinguishes between spiritualism of the East and materialism of the West? Is there thus not an indication that the Saidian text does not succeed in escaping the logic of Orientalist thought, but remains beholden to it in critiquing it?

9 Said 2003, pp. 269–70; Said 1981, p. 272.

4 Marx in the Saidian Interpretation

Marx fares far worse than Massignon in the Saidian critique, receiving none of the commendation bestowed upon the latter. What Marx's writings on the East reveal [for Said] is that Marx is only seemingly an exception to the rule and departure from Orientalist thought. Said relies on a single text of Marx to make his argument in a confident manner devoid of any doubt. He reads Marx's statement with the same analytical logic that guides his general approach to Orientalism and its intellectual structure. The following is Marx's text in question:

> Now, sickening as it must be to human feeling to witness those myriads of industrious patriarchal and inoffensive social organisations disorganised and dissolved into their units, thrown into a sea of woes, and their individual members losing at the same time their ancient form of civilisation and hereditary means of subsistence, we must not forget that these idyllic village communities, inoffensive though they may appear, had always been the solid foundation of Oriental despotism, that they restrained the human mind with the smallest possible compass, making it the unresisting tool of superstition, enslaving it beneath the traditional rules, depriving it of all grandeur and historical energies …
>
> England, it is true, in causing a social revolution in Hindustan was actuated only by the vilest of interests, and was stupid in her manner of enforcing them. But that is not the question. The question is, can mankind fulfil its destiny without a fundamental revolution in the social state of Asia? If not, whatever may have been the crimes of England, she was the unconscious tool of history in bringing about that revolution.
>
> Then, whatever bitterness the spectacle of the crumbling of an ancient world may have for our personal feelings, we have the right, in point of history, to exclaim with Goethe:
>
> Should this torture then torment us
> Since it brings us greater pleasure?
> Were not through the rule of Timur
> Souls devoured without measure?[10]

This excerpt, as we can see, comprises three paragraphs. In the first and second, Marx outlines his view of the historical relationship between English colonial-

10 Editor's note: See Karl Marx's dispatch to the *New York Daily Tribune* titled 'The British Rule in India', 25 June 1853.

ism and India, as well as the effects of this relationship on the Indian social structure. In the third paragraph, he supports this view with a verse from Goethe. A sound reading of this passage would contextualise this quote [from Goethe] by considering its meaning in light of what was said before it, i.e. the content of the first two paragraphs, as this content determines the meaning of the quote and not vice versa.

What does Marx say in these paragraphs? If the reader were to ask himself this question, which we would also pose to the author of *Orientalism*, he would look for the answer in the paragraphs written by Marx rather than what he quotes of Goethe. Inverting the relationship between text and quotation distorts both. Yet, Edward Said's reading hinges on this very inversion. Indeed, his interpretation of the Marxian text drops its first two paragraphs and leaves nothing of the third save for Goethe's verse, which he removes from its context in Marx's thought to place in the context of his own thought, where they take on a meaning different from that which it has in its original context. In such an interpretation, Marx is eclipsed by Goethe, and Said is content to use the latter's poetry to understand the former.

If we return to the original [Marxian] text, we see the objective dialectical movement characteristic of historical materialism in the first two paragraphs, specifically in their discussion of the dissolution of 'patriarchal social organisations' in India under the aegis of English colonialism and capitalist expansion. In this discussion, Marx disparages colonialism as 'sickening ... to human feeling'. But it is not a *descriptive* discussion, which is to say that it is not limited to describing either colonialism's destructive effects or the disgust it elicits. Rather, this text is concerned most of all with the question explicitly raised [in the second paragraph]: 'Can mankind fulfil its destiny without a fundamental revolution in the social state of Asia?' The central issue at the heart of Marx's text is this question of revolution and its necessity as a condition for human liberation in Asia.

If we were to read the first paragraph of this text in a calm and reasonable manner, we would see that, [according to Marx], 'the patriarchal social organisations' which 'had always been the solid foundation of Oriental despotism' and depleted 'its historical energies' stand in the way of this liberation. This means that the liberation of history through which humankind itself is liberated requires, by historical necessity, the demolition of these societies. There is no means for history and humankind to escape this necessity – which is in history, the necessity of revolution. Marx considers the movement of Asian societies' demolition and breakdown out of concern with the objective trajectory of historical necessity, and not from a position of *ethical* or *humanist* thinking. This concern also informs his assessment of the relationship between this movement and British colonialism whereby he identifies England as 'the unconscious tool of history in bringing about that revolution'. It is worth noting here that the Arabic translation of this phrase is inaccurate. The original English does not speak of the 'successful achievement of the revolution' mentioned in the Arabic. Rather, the English [verbal noun] in this passage is 'to bring about'.[11] If not for the distortion of the Marxian text in its Saidian interpretation, we would not have alluded to this [discrepancy], but the imprecise Arabic translation of this phrase fits into this interpretation. There is a huge difference between bringing about revolution and accomplishing it. It is the very same difference that separates a material, objective movement of history – which establishes the new in its destruction of the old itself – from an *intentional* movement of history. The latter is characteristic of the idealist conception of history, which eliminates the material contradiction at its core as though history is the movement of 'regenerating a fundamentally lifeless Asia', a phrase found in the Saidian interpretation [quoted below].[12] There is thus a huge difference between [the reading of] England as 'the unconscious tool of history' in the Marxian text, which situates it within an objective movement where history moves according to a dialectical material logic and thus outside of – and indeed in spite of – human consciousness and will, and the [Saidian] interpretation of England as a master [agent] of history situated within an intentional movement where history moves according to an ideological logic of Orientalist or colonialist consciousness. This is the difference between a materialist versus an idealist and subjective view of history. It is wrong to interpret the Marxian text according to the second view, as Edward Said does, especially in light of the fact that the third paragraph of this text – in which Marx invokes Goethe – affirms that he is speaking 'in point of history' and, on that note, quotes the lines of poetry. The Saidian interpretation not only drops the first two paragraphs of the text, but also drops this phrase ('in point of history') from the last paragraph, a phrase that encapsulates the meaning of the entire text and explains [Marx's understanding of] Goethe's verses.

Having pointed that out, what does the [Saidian] interpretation say? Let us read it closely. Said says:

> The quotation, which supports Marx's argument about the torment producing pleasures, comes from the *Westölicher Diwan* and identifies the sources of Marx's conceptions about the Orient. These are Romantic

11 Editor's note: The following phrase was cut from this sentence: which is rendered accordingly in the French as 'susciter'.

12 Said 2003, p. 154; Said 1981, p. 171.

and even messianic: as human material in the Orient is less important than as an element in a Romantic redemptive project. Marx's economic analyses are perfectly fitted thus to a standard Orientalist undertaking, even though Marx's humanity, his sympathy for the misery of people, are clearly engaged. Yet in the end it is the Romantic Orientalist vision that wins out, as Marx's theoretical socio-economic views become submerged in this classically standard image:

> England has to fulfill a double mission in India: one destructive, the other regenerating – the annihilation of the Asiatic society, and the laying of the material foundations of Western society in Asia.[13]

The idea of regenerating a fundamentally lifeless Asia is a piece of pure Romantic Orientalism, of course, but coming from the same writer who could not easily forget the human suffering involved, the statement is puzzling. It requires us first to ask how Marx's moral equation of Asiatic loss with the British colonial rule he condemned gets skewed back towards the old inequality between East and West we have so far remarked. Second, it requires us to ask where the human sympathy has gone, into what realm of thought it has disappeared while the Orientalist vision takes its place.[14]

5 A Moral Trial

We have intentionally quoted both the Marxian text and its Saidian interpretation in their entirety. The latter is wholly based on the former. Not one of Marx's other writings are cited in *Orientalism* to support Said's interpretation. Considering the ambition of Said's project – an ambition we may not envy – we wonder whether critique can be conducted so lightly. Rather than introducing texts by Marx unquoted in *Orientalism*, we ask the reader to simply compare the quoted Marxian excerpt with Said's interpretation of it [to judge for themselves]. In the Marxian text, the reader finds an articulation of a materialist outlook on history concerned with events and the relations between them from the standpoint of *history* and its objective movement rather than that of the *human self*. The latter would fit the Saidian theory of 'torment that brings pleasure'. Said's interpretation begins with a grave distortion not just of this particular text, but of the entire edifice of Marxist thought. This is because Said

13 Marx 1973, pp. 306–7.

14 Said 2003, p. 154; Said 1981, p. 171.

denies the *materialist basis* on which this thought rests and thereby denies its *revolutionary newness* against all thought which preceded it. That Said distorts Marx's text to this degree should give pause to anyone familiar with the ABCs of Marxism. First among these ABCs is the notion of history as a materialist movement governed by objective laws that determine the necessity of revolutionary change therein. For Marx, history is not governed by the human will but vice versa. Said's text does not acknowledge the novelty of this idea. Perhaps he is unaware of (or wilfully ignorant) of just how new this idea was, and that Marx's concept of revolution stood against all idealist metaphysical concepts that posited revolution as a romantic Christian project to save the human soul.

The idea that Marxist thought is somehow based in Christian sources – and that its revolution is a version of the Christian [salvific] project – is a familiar theory as old as crisis-ridden bourgeois imperialist ideology and is part of the latter's struggle against revolutionary thought. I do not think any serious contemporary scholar continues to accept it. Why then does the author of *Orientalism* so eagerly and wholly give preference to this theory? Our previous and subsequent critiques of Said hold the answer. Our purpose here is to point out how Said's interpretation bears not only on 'Marx's conception of the Orient', but on the totality of Marxist theory. In denying its materialist character, Said denies its revolutionary newness and consequently its antagonistic contradiction with dominant bourgeois thought. His interpretation thus enables the incorporation [of Marxian thought] into the theoretical structure of dominant bourgeois thought and as one of its elements. By reiterating this implicit epistemic basis [of bourgeois thought], this interpretation affirms that individual thought, including Marx's, is incapable of transcending the dominant thought of the nation to which the individual belongs. As such, dominant nationalist thought occupies the entire spectrum of thinking. If other thought were to exist, then the logic of nationalist thought as rendered by the Saidian interpretation would necessitate that it exist within the confines of dominant thought and as an element of it, no matter if this other thought attempts to transcend dominant thought or not. In such a scheme, revolution loses its historical necessity. Instead, it could only ever be a romantic project prevalent in the annals of dominant thought – a Christian project of saving the human spirit through purifying torment necessary for pleasure – dispersed throughout the various literatures of dominant thought.

CHAPTER 7

The Islamised Bourgeois Trend

Book Title:
A Critique of Everyday Thought[1]
Beirut: Dar al-Farabi, 2011. (First published in 1988).

Part IV The Islamised Bourgeois Trend

The Contradiction in Islam Is between Those Who Defer to Power and Those Who Defy It

The use of the charge of atheism as a weapon against those opposed to power does not mean, as power's faithful servants – including [Islamic] jurists – love to claim, that the primary contradiction in Islam is between belief and atheism. It also does not mean that belief or religion is for those in power while atheism is for those who defy it. Reality disproves such a simplification, which might be held true only by those in power and among its ruling classes. Perhaps because of its simplicity, some scholars of Islamic intellectual history have taken to this idea, or have at least been tempted by it. They have asserted that the defining contradiction in Islamic thought is that between religion and reason. Where religion was given primacy over reason, such as in the thought of al-Ghazali, they saw reactionism. Where reason prevailed, by contrast, they saw progressivism. They thus treated reason as a monolithic category, indivisible by the contradiction between, for example, the following two modes of reasoning: that of dominant reason in a despotic regime – best expressed in Islamic jurisprudence (*fiqh*), i.e. the reason of religious law – and a reason antithetical to it.

Perhaps we cannot speak of a distinctly antithetical reason in a despotic system in the same sense that proletarian reason is distinct from bourgeois reason in a capitalist system. [In the case of Islamic thought], we may very well find this contradiction between two opposing forms of reason in the thought of a single thinker, as is true for Averroes. It is even clearer in the thought of Ibn Khal-

1 Editor's note: This book was published posthumously based on an unfinished manuscript that Amel had begun writing in 1980. The manuscript's main title is Amel's. But the chapter divisions and subdivisions, as well as their respective titles, were devised by the committee entrusted with preserving his works.

 | DOI:10.1163/9789004444249_008

dun, specifically in the contradiction therein between a novel form of reason in Islamic thought, namely scientific reason [introduced by Ibn Khaldun], and another form of reason prevalent in the politics of Salafi legal reasoning [that Ibn Khaldun also practiced].[2] One cause that prevented this exceptional, independent antithetical reason to form might have been the fact that the contradictory forms of reasoning we find in Islamic thought remained part of a single logical paradigm, that of religious thought. Another related cause is the fact that the direct antithesis of dominant reason [in despotic regimes in Islamic history] was not another form of reason. Rather, it was illuminationist Sufi thought, which is a refutation and absolute rejection of reason that does not distinguish between dominant reason and the reason which opposed it. The material conditions for refuting the former are none other than the conditions for revolution against and transformation of the system of despotism [that this reason supports]. These conditions may not have ripened [during the historical period under study]. As a result, rejecting and refuting the despotic order was embodied in thought opposed to reason *in toto* rather than in thought capable of producing another form of reason opposed to dominant reason. In light of the complicated nature of the contradiction [in Islamic thought], we must take a closer look at Sufi thought and its critique.

The primary contradiction in Islam was not between belief and atheism, but between a spiritual Islam and a temporal Islam.[3] It is not, therefore, between

---

2 See Amel 1984.

3 To aid our discussion of this point, I cite a long excerpt from my article, 'On the Methods of Arabic Philosophy and General Philosophy, Respectively', published in *al-Tariq*, no. 9, October 1968. There, I say:

> In Arab thought, there is a radical conflict between two major historical currents: rationalist and illuminationist. The rationalist current emerges from a particular conception of Islam epitomized in the thought of Averroes and present in the Mu'tazalites and al-Ghazali. The illuminationist current emerges from another understanding of Islam visible in the thought of al-Hallaj, Suhrawardi, Ibn 'Arabi and other imams of Sufism. The primary issue around which this intellectual conflict revolves is *tawhid* [God's unity] and how to understand it. Both trends affirm the absolute oneness of God, albeit with different ways of conceptualizing it that yield different theoretical and practical conclusions. Starting with an absolute transcendence (*tanzih*) of God, the rationalist current affirms that all we can say about God is that he exists (*mawjud*), and that there is no way of comprehending (*idrak*) him. This statement contains a social indicator: it defines Islam as Islamic law alone, i.e. as a social system of governance. This system derives its sanctity directly from God as a completely transcendental existence. There is no room for doubt in God or for revolution against him in this system because the holiness of the *shari'a* lies in the fact that its foundation is completely abstracted from man, submitting neither to his rule nor to his comprehension. Thus *shari'a* became the ideology of the ruling class in Islamic society, i.e. of an Arab aristocratic class. This ideological definition of Islam as *shari'a* appeared clearly in Averroes, especially in his *Decisive Treatise* (*Fasl al-Maqal*). The rationalist cur-

religion and earthly life, but between two different concepts of religion itself: one in which the spiritual prevails over the temporal, and another in which the temporal totally prevails over the spiritual. The first is illuminationist, Sufi Islam, while the second is juridical, legal Islam. We have already alluded to this and analysed some of its aspects. What we mean to emphasise here is how Islam, in the course of time, sided – overall – with the ruling classes by furnishing them with a weapon against whoever called into question the legitimacy of their rule and revolted against their power, aspiring to demolish its foundations and change it. This is social rather than a religious claim and thereby affords exceptions. Laws governing society or history are generalisations. Actual events, phenomena, or realities that contradict this law actually affirm it. They delineate the limits of historical material conditions under which the law is expressed, always as a contradiction.

We must therefore be precise with regards to the formulations of such laws so that they do not say one thing and its opposite. It is possible to cite examples from recent events or distant history which indicate the opposite of what we just argued and suggest instead that Islam, in the course of time, has not in fact served the ruling classes and their [political] system, but, conversely, has worked in favour of those who revolted against the ruling classes. One could cite [the role of Islam] in Algeria's war for national liberation, for example, or in Lebanon under the Israeli occupation. These two and other examples, however, do not negate what we have said. Indeed, these examples affirm that the exception proves the rule. Simply put, they also affirm that Islam – and religion in general – is not in and of itself 'reactionary' or 'progressive', just as it is not

rent in Islam appears to us as an attempt to 'rationalize' the rule of an Arab aristocracy to create a 'theoretical' basis for its despotic rule. The 'progressiveness' of this rationalist thought also has its 'reactionary' face. We must bring this face to light in order to behold Arabic thought with a critical eye rather than to praise it, and to connect this thought to the social structure it mirrors.

Like its rationalist counterpart, the illuminationist current also begins with the absolute de-anthropomorphization of God. This current, however, revolts against this de-anthropomorphization in the way it understands God's oneness (*tawhid*). Its way of affirming the oneness of God is a subversion of divine reality as completely abstract. This form of affirmation it takes is in fact a theoretical expression of this thought's rejection of the social reality of despotism. Such a revolution against the society of despotism could only be expressed in Sufi thought because all real attempts at revolution had failed. Sufi thought is a reflection of this failure, which both determined this thought and was determined by it. It is the proof and expression of this rejection, that was incapable of ever actualizing itself.

I did not change a word of this passage, even though some of its claims should be tempered and some of its phrases made more precise.

revolutionary or anti-revolutionary. This is not to say that these categorisations or definitions, given their political character, do not apply to Islam. Nor is it to say that they do not apply because Islam inhabits an otherworldly or absolute position that rises above each and every conflict. Rather, such claims are only possible in relation to how Islam unfolds in time, in accordance with this or that opposing force of the social struggle. The unfolding of Islam in time situates it in the political class struggle that is raging within an actual and specific [political] order during a specific time and under [specific] historical conditions. At any given time, Islam's character reflects both the position it occupies in this struggle and the particular social force that appropriates it. Islam's actualisation in time is precisely its material historical existence, in which it, i.e. Islam, exists as a field of the class struggle that is renewed so long as the conditions for its regeneration exist. Islam's material existence rather than its otherworldly existence is what determines its revolutionary or anti-revolutionary character, which is none other than its class character. Just as Islam's temporalisation is inescapable, so is its occupation of a position in the class struggle, where its class character is determined. It is natural and indeed necessary that Islam's position would be multiple rather than singular – even as it is singular on an otherworldly level – due to the multiplicity of the conflicting social forces that put Islam to use. It is also natural that it would occupy contradictory positions, as per the contradiction between these forces. Never in history have these forces [of Islam] been singular, even when they constituted a nation (*umma*). Moreover, Islam was an *umma* only according to one, among many, particular interpretations, namely that of its dominant juridical interpretation. It was also an *umma* only in Islamic Jurisprudence – not in material social reality. According to the latter, the *umma* was divided into different, conflicting factions and parties (classes). It is unscientific and an annulment of knowledge to analyse reality, and by extension the *umma*, through the lens of *fiqh* (i.e. as this jurisprudence had shaped and adopted it) rather than through the lens of material history. It is equally unscientific and an annulment of knowledge to project the theological concept of the *umma* onto actual history. As such, history and *fiqh* become synonymous, and history in its material reality must conform to Islamic jurisprudence. The jurists see it this way, as do their Islamist protégés who are engaged in today's class struggle.[4]

4 For an example of this, see al-Sayyid 1980.

On the Difference between Islam's Temporalisation and Its Institutionalisation

To put it more precisely, perhaps it is better to say the following: As Islam was institutionalised (i.e. turned into an institution), it turned into an authoritarian apparatus (*jihaz sultawi*) or, to use one of Althusser's terms, an ideological state apparatus. In its institutionalisation – not its temporalisation – Islam sided with the ruling classes and the system of their class rule. This is true of religion in general as was the case for instance of Christianity's institutionalisation in the Church, which is the form of power (i.e. state form) taken by its temporalisation. Even if certain [institutionalised] currents of Islam resisted siding with the ruling classes, their attempts to do so were doomed to fail. This is because the very logic of Islam's institutionalisations, i.e. of it becoming Islamic jurisprudence (*fiqh*) or Islamic law (*sharʿ*), objectively necessitated that it be affiliated with the ruling classes. By contrast, for Islam to be on the side of the classes opposed to the ruling class within the socio-political contradiction at hand, it must stand in contradiction and conflict with institutionalised Islam. This institutionalised Islam is the Islam of the ruling classes, whose system is run by officers of the law.

In other words, it is the antagonistic contradiction between the toiling classes on one hand and the ruling class on the other that situates the former's Islam in a conflictual relation with the latter's. This relation of contradiction between the two Islams – in their active imbrication in the social contradiction between the toiling classes and their class practices on hand and the ruling classes and their class practices on the other – is what determines the former as a non-institutional (if not anti-institutional) Islam while determining the latter as an institutional Islam. It is here where we may be able to glean the real meaning of the saying that there is no clergy in Islam. Unsurprisingly, Islam's 'legalist' current understands this saying in its superficial, popular sense, namely that Islam does not impose chastity on holy men by prohibiting them to marry, nor does it require their complete self-dedication to God. In this understanding, 'no clergy in Islam' is purely about sex and the absolute contradiction between religion and the world. The believer must therefore choose, in absolute terms, religion – and as a logical consequence monasticism (*rahbana*) – or this-worldly life. The significance of this claim in Islam – and Christianity – lies elsewhere. First and foremost, it is a rejection of Islam's institutionalisation along the lines of Christianity's institutionalisation in the Church. Islam's 'legalist' current strove to eradicate this signification, which we must bring to light. Islam was temporalised [i.e. actualised through time], but in many forms that differed according to its position in the social struggle and the specific historical conditions of this conflict. Institutional Islam is the distinct historical form in which Islam was temporalised from the ruling classes' point of view. It is one and the same as the juridical 'legalist' form by which Islam was fused with the state, thus creating the Islamic state not in the general sense fancifully conjured by the ruling classes and their ideology, but as the state of these particular ruling classes. Only by *fiqh* did this Islamic state come to be.

In tangible historical reality, however, this state was never as it existed by and in *fiqh*, even at the beginning of its historical formation during the era of the Rightly-Guided Caliphs. The third caliph, 'Uthman bin 'Affan, for example, was killed in a popular revolt against oppression and the monopolisation of power by a tribal and class elite. The Umayyads thus established the first state in Islam (the Umayyad state) and gave Islamic society its class character. From the historical perspective of the state, the establishment of a hereditary state was a positive development. But it should also be noted that the state, Islamic or otherwise, could only have arisen on and through the consecration of social disparity that necessarily takes a class character, regardless of the bourgeois ideological analysis that neglects to portray it in class terms. Engels confirms this by connecting state formation, generally speaking, with the emergence of a class society and the establishment of a monopoly by the society's highest social faction of surplus social production, whereby the state becomes the tool of class dominance by the ruling class.

This is also confirmed in another language which strives to separate itself from the Marxist conceptual lexicon by removing the word 'class' and its derivatives from its vocabulary. This language, namely that of contemporary political 'science', used by Georges Balandier and others who are never suspected of espousing Marxism. Balandier links state formation to social disparity and defines one aspect of the state's function to be its necessary preservation of both this conflict and the standing system, along with the balanced disparity it guarantees. It is nonetheless also true that the state in Islam – from the time of the Umayyads up to the late Ottomans, which includes the 'Abbasids, Seljuks, Mamluks, and others – was nothing other than a state in which ruling classes took turns governing without any essential change to the mode and relations of production. It was a despotic state based on a relatively stable material basis of relations of production characterised by the absence of private property in relation to its means of production, especially land. Marx incidentally alluded to this in his concept of an 'Asiatic mode of production'. Marxist thinkers have since attempted to grasp this through a reinvigorated analysis of the 'Asiatic mode of production', which has generated intense, ongoing debate.

We will not get into this discussion now, as it is far from the subject at hand. Instead, what we want to argue is that it is a mistake to characterise the state in Islamic history as Islamic. This would only be true if an Islamic state and a despotic state were one and the same thing. This is true if institutional Islam *alone* is Islam. Islamic jurists of the 'legalist' current, whose function is almost entirely relegated to justifying the practices of power and furnishing the despotic state with legitimacy, understood it this way. So do current day would-be jurists who adhere to Islamised thought. For yesterday's jurists and today's would-be jurists alike, it is as though the state of absolute despotism, in its actual historical reality as an Umayyad, Abbasid, or Ottoman state ... is the model for the Islamic state. Or conversely, it is as though the Islamic state is an absolute and otherworldly archetype that is repeatedly actualised throughout history in different forms, which by *fiqh* alone, are but an iteration of the archetype they aspire to emulate. The internal logic of this conformance of historical forms to an archetype leads to the following: Firstly, reducing Islam to *fiqh* whereby the latter is the theo-legal reason of the state. Secondly, institutionalising Islam in the process of its becoming an Islam of the state. According to this logic, any kind of defiance of the state or authority, i.e. against the *status quo*, is a defiance of Islam itself. It is as though Islam's only purpose is to furnish the system of class despotism, in all its historical manifestations, with a suitable framework for its perpetual renewal, which is none other than Islam in its institutional form.

We can thus say with a level of certainty that the institutional form of Islam's temporalisation is what gives Islam a conservative, if not reactionary, character that reflects the political and ideological practices of the ruling classes. Under specific historical and material conditions, this Islam of the ruling classes is thus rendered an obstacle in the path of revolutionary change. It therefore becomes possible and natural for such a revolutionary movement to take on a *religious* Islamic character and that, under particular historical conditions, it would run up against institutional Islam. In this case, it is the revolutionary movement which represents Islam, and institutional Islam which defies it. This can be seen in many revolutionary movements. The Qarmatians is a case in point. Under particular circumstances, their movement had a religious Islamic character and opposed institutional Islam, the latter being the Islam of the despotic state. It can also be seen in many of the current revolutionary movements against institutional Islam such as the one adopted by Sudanese President Gaafar Nimeiry, or that of the oil princes, their entourage and harem.

Islam's Temporalisation Is Its Politicisation

The class character of Islam is thus not defined in the realm of otherworldliness, but in the field of the political struggle according to the position that it occupies therein. Islam is politicised in time. Politically speaking then, Islam is not the standard that defines the course of struggle, just as it does not have a particular [class] character affiliated with one party or another in this struggle. This struggle, which is a class struggle (let us call it by its name!) is not defined by metaphysics. Rather, the metaphysical – in the many different ways it relates to social consciousness – is defined by class struggle. Indeed, if the institutional form of Islam is the form that it takes in the course of time as it turns into a system of rule from the standpoint of the ruling classes, then the *spiritual* form, particularly the Sufi-Illuminationist form, is the historical form that it takes from the standpoint of rejecting and overturning despotic rule. This is true even if the downtrodden classes did not see Islam's spiritual form as 'their Islam'. These classes might have generally identified Islam's ruling institutional form as their Islam. This is because the social contradiction is not determined in social consciousness, but in objective social existence. This existence, moreover, is what determines social consciousness or, to use Marx's phrase, it is not the consciousness of men that determines their existence, but their social existence that determines their consciousness. The predominance of institutional Islam indicates that it was able to become the official or legitimate Islam, i.e. to represent the legitimacy of Islam, under distinct material historical conditions: these were the conditions for class struggles particular to pre-capitalist societies that are despotic in nature. From its position of power, institutional Islam appeared to general social consciousness as though it stood for Islam in an absolute sense to the exclusion of all other forms. Even in the consciousness of the downtrodden, institutional Islam appeared to be 'their' Islam, even if in its institutional existence it represented only the Islam of the dominant.

This compels us to revise our former conclusion so as to state it more precisely: The primary contradiction in Islam, as it unfolded in time and institutions, was not between belief and atheism because it was not a religious contradiction at all. Rather, its principal contradiction was a *political contradiction* enacted primarily as a religious contradiction. In other words, it was a political contradiction that unfolded as a religious contradiction for the particular historical reasons we have outlined. It was a political contradiction between, on the one hand, institutional Islam which predominated under the despotic regime, and, on the other hand, the spiritual Islam found in Sufism and its likes that was antithetical to the Islam of the despotic state. The contradiction is not, therefore, between the spiritual and the temporal, but between the temporal that is also institutional, i.e. attached to the state, and another, opposite temporal that was antagonistic to the state.

The common practice of distinguishing between spiritual and temporal power is, therefore, false. Every spiritual power is necessarily temporal and thus political due to the fact that it is *power*. Distinguishing between the two is never correct, and only appears so to the ruling classes because their interest lies in concealing religion's particular class character. This concealment does not take place in the realm of the absolute or the otherworldly, but in relation to those classes' position in the class struggle and its ideological employment of religion. The purpose of distinguishing between the temporal and spiritual is to erase the distinction in religion itself, in this case Islam, between two temporal Islams, i.e. between the revolutionary Islam and the anti-revolutionary Islam.

The phrase 'political Islam' is a logical outcome of this practice of distinguishing between temporal and spiritual Islam. It is obvious that Islam, like other religions, would have a political nature. The problem that we must address is not whether Islam is political (temporal) or not (and thus spiritual). The problem that we must not only confront but also resolve is how to define Islam's political position. The problem, in other words, is as follows: To which politics are we referring when we speak about political Islam?[5] To which Islam are we referring when we talk about political Islam and the Islam of which politics? Whose Islam? What is the political character of this political Islam? The political character of Islam is not determined – as we have said – by Islam, within Islam, or Islamically, so to speak. It is determined instead by *class*, in the sense that it is determined *historically* and *materially* by its actual position in the field of conflicting class-based political practices.

5 As we have already explained, the apolitical position is characterised by the rejection of politics in an absolute or abstract sense and does not differentiate between the two parties in the central political contradiction. Anyone who speaks about political Islam in a general sense without defining the particular class character of its political being – whether revolutionary or anti-revolutionary, reactionary bourgeois or anti-bourgeois – is speaking from a dominant bourgeois position, which correlates to the apolitical position in its non-distinction and erasure of the difference between the two parties in the political contradiction. Thus these two positions are in fact two sides of a single bourgeois class position.

CHAPTER 8

The Problem of Cultural Heritage

Book Title:
A Crisis of Arab Civilisation or a Crisis of the Arab Bourgeoisies?
Beirut: Dar al-Farabi, 2002. (First published in 1974).

Chapter 6: The Problem of Arab Thought when Subjected to Scientific Logic

Section 6: The Problem of Cultural Heritage

A This Is an Intellectual Question of the Present, Not the Past

Why does Cultural Heritage (*turath*) [hereafter Heritage] pose a problem for Arab thought that it might not pose, at least in the same form, for, say, Western thought? What are the historical conditions in which this problem was posed? When we speak about 'Heritage', moreover, of which heritage, or of which body of intellectual production, are we speaking? Since we are examining the question of 'Arab thought', we will confine [our discussion of] Heritage, for methodological purposes, to its intellectual aspect.

In general, the question of Heritage refers to the intellectual output that preceded the 'Nahda'.[1] Stated more precisely, it is concerned with Arab thought that preceded the phase of imperialist permeation of our present world. This is not to say that *Nahda* thought is not part of the Heritage of Arab thought ... *Nahda* thought, however, is 'modern', meaning that its structure can only be understood in relation to the contemporary colonial social structure whose historical formation began with the onset of imperialist penetration. The Heritage question is thus a problem of the relation between thought in this contemporary social structure, and thought that preceded it in a previous social structure. It is thus perhaps more accurate to say that this is a problem of contemporary rather than past thought. This is because the relation between the two is determined by the manner in which contemporary thought relates to past thought, i.e. by the manner in which [past] thought is revealed to [present] thought, not through [the former's] own reality, but, rather, through the real-

1 Editor's note: *Nahda* refers to the Arab cultural and literary revival movement that emerged in the nineteenth century.

 | DOI:10.1163/9789004444249_009

ity of present thought itself. [Due to its existence] in this relation, thought of the past, therefore, is not defined in itself, *but by the thought of the present that defines it. The logic of this determination is necessary* because it is the logic of the present itself.

It is thus not at all possible to look into or view the past **except from the standpoint of the present**. This view of the past from the present, however, like the outlook on present social reality itself, is necessarily determined by the ideological position, and thus also by the class position, from which this view emerges. Insofar as this position is an element of an ideological field specific to social reality of the present, it is in turn defined by its contradictory relation to other ideological positions [that exist] in the structure of this particular field. We view the past, like we do the present, through the lens of class ideology. Social reality, in the past, the present or the future, is revealed to thought strictly from the standpoint of a class ideology which itself is defined by the structure of the ideological field [existing in] the social reality of the present. This ideological field is constituted by the ideological practices of class struggle. In this field, Arab heritage is thus a subject of the struggle between warring classes in the colonial social structure of the Arab World. [Heritage] does not exist as a problem for contemporary Arab thought except in this [ideological] field in which it undergoes a second becoming, so to speak, as a subject of contemporary thought. In this *second becoming*, then, Arab heritage is not defined *in itself* except in the form *that it comes to take*, i.e. in the form *into which it is transformed* through contemporary thought's treatment of it. The essence of Heritage is neither by itself nor by self-identification, but through contemporary thought (that takes it as a subject). This is precisely the contemporary becoming of [Heritage], or its rendering as present through the present.

This is not a movement of self-identification of Heritage as past which becomes present, nor is it a movement of its identification with the present whereby it is present as continuous past. Rather, this becoming is the movement by which [Heritage] transforms at the hands of the present, or the movement by which it transforms as a subject of modern thought, i.e. as *raw material* in the process of knowledge production, or a type of knowledge production specific to the structure of this contemporary thought. Heritage's becoming is itself the movement of the production of [contemporary] thought, namely the production of knowledge specific to its structure. It must therefore be said that Heritage's self-identification is not born of an inner movement, whether it be the movement of this thought's stagnation or ossification. Nor is it born out of a movement of repetition that leads, by itself, to a juxtaposition of this thought with present or contemporary thought. Rather, it is born out of this contemporary thought which, in its treatment of Heritage, produces Heritage, or at least reproduces it, in a form where Heritage appears as if it is essentially in stagnation, ossification, or repetition.

As we showed earlier, the form in which Heritage appears in the field of class-based ideological practices of contemporary Arab reality is none other than an effect produced, in this very field, by the ideological practice of the ruling colonial bourgeoisie. The problem of heritage is not a question of past tradition, as Heritage is not essentially a subject of its own contemplation. Rather it is a problem of this contemporary Arab thought, in which Heritage becomes a subject. Intellectual Heritage preceded imperialist permeation. It is our contemporary thought, which followed this permeation, that finds it *necessary* to define the relation that it must establish with this [pre-penetration] thought. The Heritage Question lurks in this very necessity. It is a problem for the thought whose contemporary formation began with the formation of the colonial social formation, and whose renewal is determined by the renewal of this [colonial] structure within the relation of structural dependency set by imperialism. The heritage question is thus a problem of Arab thought which, in its becoming, is in a specific historical movement, namely the movement of its national liberation. It is very important to acknowledge this in identifying the historical reasons for the emergence of [the concept of] Heritage, in contemporary Arab thought, as a problem the likes of which we might not find in contemporary European thought. It is equally important in terms of defining the historical conditions in which this problem was generated as such.

B The Historical Conditions for Posing the Problem at Hand

Imperialist permeation of the movement of historical development of Arab (and non-Arab) social formations produced a radical turn [in this movement] that brought about new relations of production. It is hard to say that they were the result of historical necessity, [in other words], that they were due to a logic of development internal to these formations prior to imperialist penetration. This is so since these relations came about as a historical result of the dismantling of past relations of production caused by imperialist penetration. The *motor force* of our modern history, then, was the imperialist development of capitalism. In the Arab World, we did not transition to our contemporary history by force of the movement of contradictions internal to our pre-capitalist social formations, but by force of imperialist domination over those formations and the dependency which bound them to that rule. With the onset of imperialist rule and our subjection to it, the *contemporary history* of our Arab World began, as did the contemporary or modern history of all social structures which, in this contemporary history of ours, is in a movement of national liberation. We came to this history by force of the same [imperialist] domination from which we must liberate ourselves in order to, in turn, liberate and seize hold of our history by seizing hold of the very necessity driving it towards liberation. Imperialism produced a rupture in the movement of our social history, a rupture where our history parted with us upon entering another movement: the renewal of the relation of structural dependency on imperialism.

Our history's movement was thus necessarily determined as a movement of self-reclamation through class struggle, which is the motor force behind the necessary logic that governs this history's movement towards transition to socialism. This *rupture* of which we are speaking is none other than the very *historical movement* in which the relation of structural dependency on imperialism was constituted; for this movement is the historical form or framework in which the Arab World transitioned from a pre-capitalist to a capitalist social formation. As we see it, then, this rupture is in fact antithetical to the concept of 'civilisational or cultural rupture' in Dr Zakariyya's paper, which presents 'the rupture' as a moment when *history stopped* in the Arab World while continuing outside of it.[2] We understand this rupture, on the contrary, to be the particular form of socio-historical movement by which the social structure transitioned – in its historical transition from one mode of production to another – to *dependent development.* Determined by relations of colonial production and by the dominating side in the structural dependency relation to imperialism, dependent development was, in the final analysis, determined by the imperialist development of capitalism. It is therefore precisely this *relationship of dependency* that produced the rupture in the history of the Arab World whereupon that world's present ceased to be part of history – so to speak – along with its past. This is so since in the final analysis, imperialist development is precisely the determining factor of this present, in its own determination by the existing structure of colonial relations of production.

In the realm of ideology, imperialist development is what determines the form in which Arab Heritage appears to dominant Arab thought. Imperialist development does so by determining the structure of dominant colonial-bourgeois ideology from and through which that heritage is viewed. Through its ideology and Orientalists, imperialism attempted in many different ways to make its domination appear as a '*civilising mission*' and thereby make the *power relation* appear as a civilisational *relation.* In this way, the logic of interpreting the imperialist relation changed; the necessity of imperialist development in capitalism was no longer the cause [for this relation]. Instead, *the cause* became *the necessity of transitioning to civilisation* in these 'backwards' coun-

2 Editor's note: Dr. Zakariyya was one of the participants at the Kuwait Conference whose proceedings Amel is criticising.

tries which are facing a crisis of transitioning to civilisation.[3] According to this ideologically-driven imperialist logic, 'The civilising mission' of the West is merely a necessary effect of that cause, which is our society's inability to transition along with its self-identified Arab reason, to the civilisation, reason, and logic of the age. The crisis is thus [presumably] a crisis of this Arab civilisation, which is the cause of its own crisis because it is unable to transition to human civilisation. Humanity, meanwhile, requires of whomever arrives to this elevated stage of civilisation, in its early form or in its secondary technological form, to take whomever lags behind it by the hand. Force was necessary in the beginning. As for now, the force of argument has taken its place, for whoever lags behind progress has been convinced of the necessity of emulating whomever achieved progress. These two situations, in fact, partake in the same logic. We have seen many varied instances of it in the papers presented at the Kuwait conference.

In accordance with the ideologically-driven logic of its 'civilising message', imperialism conjured the Heritage of societies it considered necessary to absorb into its civilisation in a way that justified its 'civilizing mission' as a historical necessity in the eyes of these [colonised] societies themselves, or at least in the view of its dominant classes. Heritage became the reason for the necessity of imperialist domination. It had to appear in a form that emphasised the necessity of accepting this rule. The disparity between this heritage and imperialist rule was the very disparity between backwardness and civilisation, or between underdevelopment and progress. Heritage had thus either to persist, and in so doing prolong backwardness, or to transition to imperial dependency, which stood for progress. Imperialism had to distort the Heritage it conjured in order to make obvious, in the mind of the ruling classes in colonised societies, the choice between the following: the persistence of Heritage as the negation of civilisation, on the one hand, and civilisation as dependency [on imperialism], on the other. Indeed, this conjuring preserved specific manifestations [of Heritage] which, in the logic of imperialist ideology, was used as a means of condemning this heritage when compared to other glamorous manifestations of social reality, itself born out of this relation of dependency. Orientalism played a major role in this imperialist conjuring of Heritage, a role that found its natural and dependent extension in colonial bourgeois ideology.

The oddity is that this imperialist ideology was taken up by the bourgeois leadership of many national movements, especially during the early twentieth century. These movements wanted to convince the imperialist powers that our

3 Editor's note: In the context of speaking about culture and civilisational missions, 'backwards' seemed like a more apt translation of *takhalluf* than 'underdevelopment'.

Arab countries had become capable of ruling themselves on their own, and as a result they may transition to political independence under the auspices of these powers. The bourgeois leadership of the national movement in Egypt, for example, attended the 1919 League of Nations' Paris Conference to convince the imperialist bourgeoisie that the latter's 'civilising message' had been brought to fruition, and that Egypt then was a 'civilised' country which must, therefore, be independent. Surprised by the popular movement of 1919, Egypt's bourgeois leadership sought to unite and steer the movement so that it would appear 'civilised', and a far cry from extremism, demagoguery, and chaos, i.e. all that is antithetical to 'civilisation'. This shows us that the logic of the 'civilizing message' touted by the imperialist West had been internalised, approved, and adopted. The very same logic – albeit in a different form – is also at work in the colonial bourgeoisie's treatment of the 'crisis of Arab civilisation'.

List of Amel's Published Books

Books Published during His Lifetime

Theoretical Prolegomena to the Study of the Impact of Socialist Thought on the National Liberation Movement – Part I: On Contradiction (1973); *Part II: On the Colonial Mode of Production* (1973) (*Muqaddimat Nadhariyya li Dirasat Athar al-Fikr al-Ishtiraki fi Harakat al-Taharrur al-Watani; Al-Juz' al-Awwal: Fi al-Tanaqud; al-Juz' al-Thani: Fi Namat al-Intaj al-Kulinyali*)

A Crisis of Arab Civilisation or a Crisis of the Arab Bourgeoisies? (1974) (*Azmat al-Hadara al-Arabiyya am Azmat al-Burjwaziyyat al-Arabiyya*)

Theory in Political Practice: An Inquiry into the Causes of the [*Lebanese*] *Civil War* (1979) (*Al-Nadhariyya fi al-Mumarasa al-Siyasiyya: Bahth fi Asbab al-Harb al-Ahliyya*)

A Gateway into Refuting Sectarian Thought: The Palestinian Cause in Lebanese Bourgeois Ideology (1980) (*Madkhal ila Naqd al-Fikr al-Ta'ifi: al-Qadiyya al-Filastiniyya fi Aydyulujiyyat al-Burjwaziyya al-Lubnaniyya*)

Does the Heart Belong to the East and the Mind to the West? Marx in the Orientalism of Edward Said (1985) (*Hal al-Qalb lil Sharq wa al-'Aql lil Gharb? Marx fi Istishraq Edward Said*)

On the Scientific [*Nature*] *of Ibn Khaldoun's Thought* (1985) (*Fi 'ilmiyyat al-Fikr al-Khalduni*)

On the Sectarian State (1986) (*Fi al-Dawla al-Ta'ifiyya*)

Books Published Posthumously

A Critique of Everyday Thought (1988) (*Naqd al-Fikr al-Yawmi*)

Discussions and Conversations into the Issues of National Liberation Movement and the Particularity of Marxian Concepts Arab-wise (1990)

On Matters of Education and Teaching Policy (1991) (*Fi Qadaya al-Tarbiya wa al-Siyasa al-Ta'limiyya*)

On the Staging of History (2001) (*Fi Tamarhul al-Tarikh*)

Poetry

Temporal Improvisations (1974) (*Taqasim ala al-zaman*)
The Space of N (1984) (*Fada' al-Noon*)

All books were published by *Dar Al-Farabi* in Beirut. Dates listed are first editions. Original Arabic titles are included in between brackets.

Bibliography

Abu Rabi', Ibrahim M. 2004, *Contemporary Arab Thought: Studies in Post-1967 Arab Intellectual History*, London: Pluto Press.

al-Sayyid, Radwan 1980, 'From Peoples and Tribes to an *Umma*', *Al-Wihda*, 4 (July).

Amel, Mahdi 1968, 'On the Methods of Arabic Philosophy and General Philosophy, Respectively', *al-Tariq*, 9, 28 October.

Amel, Mahdi 1979, *Theory in Political Practice: An Inquiry into the Causes of the Lebanese Civil War*, Beirut: Dar al-Farabi.

Amel, Mahdi 1980, *A Gateway into Refuting Sectarian Thought: The Palestinian Cause in the Ideology of the Lebanese Bourgeoisie*, Beirut: Dar al-Farabi.

Amel, Mahdi 1984, *On the Scientificity of Khaldunian Thought*, Beirut: Dar al-Farabi.

Amel, Mahdi 1990, *Theoretical Prolegomena to the Study of the Impact of Socialist Thought on the National Liberation Movement*, 6th edn, Beirut: Dar al-Farabi.

Amel, Mahdi 2002, *A Crisis of Arab Civilization or a Crisis of the Arab Bourgeoisies?* Beirut: Dar al-Farabi.

Amel, Mahdi 2003, *On the Sectarian State*, 3rd edn, Beirut: Dar al-Farabi.

Amel, Mahdi 2006, *Does the Heart Belong to the East and the Mind to the West? Marx in the Orientalism of Edward Said*, 3rd edn, Beirut: Dar al-Farabi.

Amel, Mahdi 2011, *A Critique of Everyday Thought*, Beirut: Dar al-Farabi.

Amel, Mahdi 2013, *Theoretical Prolegomena to the Study of the Impact of Socialist Thought on the National Liberation Movement*, 7th edn, Beirut: Dar al-Farabi.

Anderson, Kevin B. 2010, *Marx at the Margins: On Nationalism, Ethnicity, and non-Western Societies*, Chicago: University of Chicago Press.

Bettelheim, Charles 1962, *L'Inde Independante*, Paris: Armand Colin.

Frangie, Samer 2012, 'Theorizing from the Periphery: The Intellectual Project of Mahdi "Amil"', *International Journal of Middle East Studies* 44, no. 3: 465–82.

Hamdan, Evelyne 2018, *L'Homme aux Sandales de Feu*, Beirut: Dar al-Farabi.

Marx, Karl 1904, *A Contribution to the Critique of Political Economy*, Chicago: Charles H. Kerr & Co.

Marx, Karl 1967, *Le Capital*, Paris: Éditions Sociales.

Marx, Karl 1967, *Fondements de la critique de l'économie politique*, Paris: Anthropos.

Marx, Karl 1973, *Surveys from Exile*, ed. David Fernbach, London: Pelican Books.

Marx, Karl 1982, *Capital*, Volume 1, London: Penguin.

Marx, Karl 1982, *Contribution à la critique de l'économie politique*, Paris: Éditions Sociales.

Marx, Karl 1991, *Capital*, Volume 3, London: Penguin.

Marx, Karl 1992, *Capital*, Volume 2, London: Penguin.

Marx, Karl 1993, *Grundrisse: Foundations of the Critique of Political Economy (Rough Draft)*, London: Penguin.

Massad, Joseph 2007, *Desiring Arabs*, Chicago: University of Chicago Press.

Prashad, Vijay 2014, 'The Arab Gramsci', *Frontline*, 21 March, https://frontline.thehindu.com/world-affairs/the-arab-gramsci/article5739956.ece

Said, Edward W. 1981, *Orientalism*, trans. Kamal Abu Deeb, Beirut: Mu'assasat al-Abhath al-ʿArabiya.

Said, Edward W. 2003, *Orientalism*, New York: Vintage Books.

Sing, Manfred and Miriam Younes 2013, 'The Specters of Marx in Edward Said's "Orientalism"', *Die Welt Des Islams* 53, no. 2: 149–91.

Tohme, Hisham Ghassan 2012, *Mahdi ʿAmil and Husayn Muruwwa: Locating Marxism in the Arab Context*, MA Dissertation, American University of Beirut.

Index

Africa 30, 57
agricultural production 40–41, 70–71
Algeria 10–11, 34, 37, 41, 50, 57, 75, 78–79
Althusser, Louis 8, 11
al-turath. *See* heritage, cultural
anti-colonial struggle 9–11, 33, 42
Arab Bourgeoisies 6, 8, 120
Arabic Philosophy 112, 128
Arab world 3, 6, 8, 10, 96, 121–23
Asiatic mode of production 116
atheism 7, 111–12, 118

backwardness XIV, 56, 124
Balandier, Georges 10, 116
Beirut 10–11, 120, 127–29
Bettelheim, Charles 10, 61
Bourdieu, Pierre 10
bourgeoisie 4, 30–31, 39–44, 51, 67, 70, 74, 80–81, 85–87, 91–96, 98
  colonial 38–40, 42, 44–45, 67–72, 74–75, 81, 87
  industrial 39, 43–44
  mercantile 31, 38–39, 42, 67
  national 6, 38, 42, 67, 74
British colonialism 108

capital 21–22, 24–26, 32–33, 36–37, 39, 54, 95, 128
capitalist development 30, 38, 43–44, 46, 53, 59, 62, 72, 78, 88
capitalist mode of production 4–5, 26–27, 29, 36, 46, 54, 60, 62, 76, 88
civil war 7, 11, 89–90, 92, 96, 98
class character 6, 11, 35, 91, 94, 114, 116–19
class contradictions 34, 44, 49, 51, 55, 64, 71, 81, 87
class struggle 5, 19–20, 34–35, 42–43, 49–51, 69–71, 74, 76, 87, 93, 96–97, 114, 117–19, 121, 123
colonialism 3–5, 27–28, 31–32, 34, 39–42, 49–50, 55, 59, 63, 65–72, 74, 76–79, 82, 84–85, 121–22
colonialist bourgeoisie XV, 42, 67, 70, 71, 74, 81
  See also bourgeoisie, colonial
Colonial Mode of Production (CoMP) 4–7, 11, 48, 51–52, 54–58, 60–61, 66, 71, 75, 83
colonised countries 4, 23–27, 30–34, 36–42, 46–47, 49–51, 53–54, 57–59, 61–62, 64, 67, 74–75
  underdeveloped 40–41, 54, 66
commodities 26, 28, 30–31, 36
CoMP. *See* Colonial Mode of Production
consciousness 49–50, 70, 73–74, 92, 97, 118
contradiction 4–5, 7–8, 18, 34, 41–42, 44–46, 51–52, 63–64, 70–71, 81–82, 86–87, 97, 100–101, 104, 111–15
crisis 6–7, 88, 91, 95–96, 98, 120, 124

Daher, Massoud 85
dependency 4, 8, 11, 24, 32, 58, 60–62, 66, 69, 74, 87, 122–24
Derrida, Jacques 11

Engels, Friedrich 116
exploitation 5, 30, 50, 70–72

Fanon, Frantz, XV 10
fascism 11, 89, 97
feudalism 40, 48, 57
Foucault, Michel 11
French Mandate 86

Germany 22, 41
al-Ghazali, Abu Hamid 111–12
Goethe, Johann Wolfgang von 106–8
Gramsci, Antonio 11
Gunder Frank, Andre 3, 11

hegemony 7, 90–94, 97–98
heritage VII, XII, XIV, 3, 6, 8, 105, 120–124
  Arab communist XII
  Arab thought 120
  Arabo-Islamic cultural 6
  Arab 121, 123
  cultural VII, XIV, 3, 6, 8, 120–124
  intellectual XII, 122
  pre-modern Eastern 105
  societies 124
humanity 25, 49, 51, 124

immigration 33
imperialism 4, 16, 22, 87–88, 122–24
India 10, 52, 69, 77, 100, 106–7, 109
Indonesia 69
industrial production 44, 69
Islam 6, 111–19
Islamic Jurisprudence XIV, 111, 114, 115
Islamic law XIV, 112, 115

Kataeb, *Phalanges* 89, 94–95
Kurdish question 10

labour 26, 30, 36, 45, 67
Latin America 3, 11, 30, 57
LCP (Lebanese Communist Party) 5, 10–11, 89
Lebanon 10–12, 41, 59, 73, 75, 84, 86, 88–89, 95–96, 98, 113
Lenin, V.I. 22, 48, 63–64, 83

Maronites 7, 86, 90–91, 95
Marx, Karl 3, 6, 8, 11, 18, 20–33, 36–38, 40, 46, 52–56, 59, 62–63, 69, 99–110, 127–29
Marxism-Leninism 32, 63
mode of production 4, 18, 26–27, 36, 48–49, 51–61, 75, 123

Nahda 120
Nasser, Gamal Abdel 78
Nasserism 10
national liberation 3, 5, 8, 11, 34, 49, 70, 113, 122
national liberation movement 3, 5, 15, 35, 48, 52, 127–28
national struggle 5, 34
neoliberalism 6

Orientalism 3, 99, 101–7, 109–10, 124

Palestine Liberation Organization 10
peasants 49–51, 70–74
petite bourgeoisie 4, 35, 43–45, 67–68, 71–72, 75, 80–81
Phalanges 89
Poulantzas, Nikos 11

revolution 3, 5, 30, 33–34, 51, 58, 66, 77, 97, 106–8, 110, 112–13
Romero, Carlos 11
ruling classes 7, 72, 74–76, 111–13, 115–18, 124
Russia 48

Said, Edward 6, 8, 99, 101–2, 105, 107–8, 127, 129
Salafi 112
Samir Amin 3
sectarianism 3, 7–8, 84–85, 87–88
sectarian state 7, 84–85, 87, 89, 91–97, 127–28
Shafiq al-Hout 10
shariʿa 112
Shia 7, 86, 94
socialism 5, 11, 30, 51, 77–78, 123
social production 41, 44, 56, 60–62, 69–70, 73, 76, 79, 81–83, 116
state 8, 36, 45, 58, 74, 79, 86, 89–96, 104, 116–18
Syria 79

Third World countries 3, 33, 76–77
turath. See heritage, cultural

Umayyads 116–17
umma 100, 114
underdevelopment 3, 5, 8–11, 15–25, 29–33, 35, 37–39, 43, 45, 47–49, 51–57, 61, 65–67, 71–73, 124

Zionism 94

Printed in the United States
By Bookmasters